Collins

Student Support
Materials for
AQA A2 Psychology

Unit 3

Topics in Psychology:
Biological Rhythms and Sleep

Author: Mike Cardwell with Simon Green
Series editor: Mike Cardwell with Alison Wadeley

Published by Collins Education
An imprint of HarperCollins*Publishers*
77–85 Fulham Palace Road
Hammersmith
London
W6 8JB

Browse the complete Collins Education catalogue at www.collinseducation.com

10 9 8 7 6 5 4 3 2 1

ISBN 978-0-00-742160-2

Mike Cardwell and Simon Green assert their moral rights to be identified as the authors of this work.

British Library Cataloguing in Publication Data.
A catalogue record for this publication is available from the British Library.

Commissioned by Charlie Evans and Andrew Campbell
Project managed by Shirley Wakley
Editorial: Hugh Hillyard-Parker
Design and typesetting by G Brasnett, Cambridge
Cover design by Angela English
Production by Simon Moore
Printed and bound by L.E.G.O. S.p.A. Italy
Indexed by Christine Boylan

Acknowledgements

Every effort has been made to contact the holders of copyright material, but if any have been inadvertently overlooked the publishers will be pleased to make the necessary arrangements at the first opportunity.

Credits and permissions

p. 6 (Study), Pengelley, E.T. & Fisher, K.C. (1957), 'Onset and cessation of hibernation under constant temperature and light in the golden-mantled ground squirrel (*Citellus lateralis*)', *Nature* 180: 1371–2, Nature Publishing Group; p.10 (Study), Siffre, M. (1975) *Dans les abîmes de la terre*, Flammarion; p. 14 (Study), Recht, L., Lew, R.A. & Schwartz, W.J. (1995), 'Baseball teams beaten by jet lag', *Nature* 377: 583, Nature Publishing Group; p. 18 (Study), Czeisler, C.A., Moore-Ede M.C. and Coleman, R.H. (1982), 'Rotating shift work schedules that disrupt sleep are improved by applying circadian principles', *Science*, 217 (4558): 460–3, American Association for the Advancement of Science; p. 19 (Study), Coren, S. (1996), *Sleep Thieves*, New York: Free Press; p. 21 (Study), Aserinsky, E. & N. Kleitman (1953), 'Regularly occurring periods of eye motility and concomitant phenomena during sleep', *Science* 118: 273–4, American Association for the Advancement of Science; p. 22 (Study) Dement, W. & Kleitman, N. (1957), 'The relation of eye movements during sleep to dream activity: an objective method for the study of dreaming', *Journal of Experimental Psychology*, 53, 339–46, American Psychological Association; p. 24 (Study), Ohayon, M.M., Carskadon, M.A., Guilleminault, C., & Vitiello, M.V. (2004), 'Meta-analysis of quantitative sleep parameters from childhood to old age in healthy individuals: developing normative sleep values across the human lifespan', *Sleep*, 27, 1255–73, American *Sleep* Disorders Association; p. 26–7 (Study), Meddis, R. (1975), 'On the function of sleep', *Journal of Animal Behavior*, 23 (3): 676–91, Elsevier; p. 28 (Study), Oswald, I. (1980), 'Sleep as a restorative process: human cues', *Progress in Brain Research*, 53: 279–88, Elsevier; p. 35 (Study), Overeem, S. *et.al.* (2008), 'Narcolepsy: immunological aspects', *Sleep Medicine Reviews* 12: 95–107, Elsevier.

Illustrations and photographs

Cover and p. 1, © Greg Hargreaves/gettyimages.co.uk; p. 21, © BSIP VEM/Science Photo Library; p. 24 (Fig. 2), adapted from Ohayon, M.M., Carskadon, M.A., Guilleminault, C., & Vitiello, M.V. (2004).

For Jane Willson

Contents

Different biological rhythms

The living world is full of biological rhythms. The evening primrose opens its flowers as darkness falls every day, while some beach-living algae burrow into the sand and emerge in rhythm with the tides. The most obvious rhythm in animals is the sleep/waking cycle, but there are many others. Some involve behaviour, but there are also physiological processes that show rhythmic activity. These include body temperature and the release of **hormones**.

Types of biological rhythm

Biological rhythms can be classified into various categories based on their periodicity or duration of their cycle.

Circadian rhythms

'Circadian' means 'about a day', and **circadian rhythms** occur with one full cycle every 24 hours. The most studied example is the human sleep/waking cycle, in which we sleep for around eight hours in every 24. Many circadian rhythms, such as body temperature, show one peak (in the afternoon) and one trough (in the early morning) every 24 hours. Far more research has been done into circadian rhythms than into any other of the biological rhythms.

Infradian rhythms

Infradian rhythms last for longer than one day. Examples include:

- the human female menstrual cycle, with a periodicity of 28 days
- hibernation in some animals such as bears and squirrels, which takes place on an annual basis – they prepare for hibernation, for example, by laying down extra layers of fat.

Ultradian rhythms

Ultradian rhythms have a cycle length of less than one day – in other words, there is more than one complete cycle in 24 hours. Examples include:

- the patterning of human meals
- the alternation between **NREM** and **REM** sleep during a night's sleep (see pp. 22–3).

Control of biological rhythms

The key feature of biological rhythms is that they show remarkable consistency, and one of the most fascinating areas of research looks at how this consistency is achieved. In some cases, it looks obvious. We go to sleep when it goes dark, and we awake when it becomes light. Animals hibernate when winter approaches, so we might assume that the key signals are the shortening of the days and/or the colder temperatures.

However, squirrels kept in a laboratory in a constant, warm environment, with alternating 12-hour periods of light and dark, still went through their hibernation routine at the appropriate time of year, increasing food intake and body weight and decreasing body temperature (Pengelley and Fisher 1957). They also awoke as spring approached in the world outside.

The evening primrose opens its flowers in the evening, and will do this at the appropriate time even when kept in constant light. These observations suggest that there must be some internal biological control that interacts with outside stimuli such as light and temperature.

Endogenous pacemakers

Observations of animals and plants have led to the suggestion that biological rhythms are inbuilt or endogenous, probably representing a genetically inherited mechanism (see below). As their role is to control biological rhythms, they are referred to as **endogenous pacemakers**, or, more simply, biological or **body clocks**.

As there are many biological rhythms, there are potentially many biological clocks. However, a major brain structure that appears to function as a key biological clock is the **suprachiasmatic nucleus (SCN)** in the **hypothalamus**. We look at the SCN later in relation to circadian rhythms (see pp. 8–9).

Body clock genes
There is a genetic component in the biological clock, first identified in the 1970s by Konopka and Benzer in their experiments using fruit flies. The first mammalian clock gene was discovered by Joseph Takahashi in 1994.

PERIOD3 (or PER3 in short) is one of the clock genes that influence the characteristics of our biological rhythms. This gene comes in different forms, and each form seems to produce a slightly different circadian pattern. This helps to explain individual variation in people's body clocks that determine, for example, whether you are a long or short sleeper, or a 'morning type' or an 'evening type' of person.

Issues, debates and approaches (IDA)

- *Research using non-human animals* – Research into brain mechanisms underlying biological clocks often involves non-human animals, raising issues of generalizing findings to humans. However, although there may be differences in detail, biological clocks seem to be similar across species.

Exogenous zeitgebers

The purpose of biological rhythms is to coordinate physiological and behavioural activities with the outside world. They make sure that animals sleep when activity is difficult and hibernate when feeding becomes impossible during the winter months. To do this effectively, the biological clocks must be synchronized with the outside world – in other words, they must respond to **exogenous** ('external') stimuli, such as light and temperature.

These external stimuli are called exogenous **zeitgebers** (from the German for 'time giver'), and the most important zeitgeber is light. We study the role of zeitgebers in relation to circadian rhythms on pp. 8–9.

Examiners' notes

'Endogenous pacemakers' is rather a mouthful, and you will see them referred to more simply as 'biological clocks' or 'body clocks' in textbooks and articles. Although use of accurate terminology is the best way to demonstrate effective learning in exam answers, use of any of these terms would be acceptable.

Essential notes

The study of clock genes is ongoing, but offers real potential for uncovering more about the physiological and molecular mechanisms involved in our body clocks.

Examiners' notes

Examiners are aware that IDA may be less available in some areas. For instance, in relation to biological rhythms, gender or cultural biases are not relevant.

Endogenous pacemakers and exogenous zeitgebers

The fundamental control of biological rhythms appears to lie in endogenous or inbuilt (innate) pacemakers, more familiarly known as body clocks. Even plants such as the evening primrose must contain cells within them with an inbuilt rhythm of activity that allows them to function as such a clock, thereby controlling when it opens and closes its flowers.

As complex animals also show a range of biological rhythms, they too must possess clocks that regulate these rhythmic activities.

The suprachiasmatic nucleus (SCN)

The SCN in the brains of mammals has been the most studied of all the biological pacemakers. The SCN is a small cluster of neurons (brain cells) in the hypothalamus, buried deep in the brain. These neurons have an intrinsic activity rhythm that persists even if the SCN neurons are isolated from the rest of the brain. If the SCN in normal animals is lesioned (damaged through cutting), the circadian rhythms of sleep/waking, body temperature and feeding patterns are totally disrupted (Stephan and Zucker 1972), showing the SCN's importance as a biological pacemaker.

Light and the SCN
Under normal circumstances, biological rhythms are synchronized with the outside world, with light being one of the key zeitgebers. Research has shown how this interaction between light and the SCN works.

The main neural pathway from the retina at the back of the eye (the retina contains the visual receptor cells) eventually runs to the visual cortex at the back of the brain, where the early stages of visual processing take place. However another, much smaller, pathway connects the retina to the SCN. This pathway is known as the **retinohypothalamic tract**. Through this pathway, the SCN receives information about the amount of light reaching the retina from the outside world, and the activity of SCN neurons can be affected by light.

Light and melatonin production
The SCN is connected in turn by a pathway that runs to the **pineal gland**, buried deep in the brain. The SCN regulates the activity of the pineal gland, whose major function is to convert the **neurotransmitter** chemical **serotonin** into the hormone **melatonin**. Melatonin is released from the pineal gland into the circulatory system and has actions on many structures in the brain and body. In particular, it seems to influence many rhythmic activities. For instance, melatonin can produce sleep in sparrows (Abraham *et al.* 2000), probably by an action on the brain's sleep mechanisms.

Release of melatonin from the pineal gland in mammals is ultimately under the control of the SCN. As light fades in the evening, the SCN responds by increasing the secretion of melatonin. Then, as night ends and dawn breaks, the increase in light stimulates the SCN to decrease melatonin secretion. This decrease in melatonin levels has been shown to be responsible for waking in chickens (Binkley 1979).

The SCN–pineal system in mammals

The SCN–pineal system in mammals has been shown through research studies to be one of the brain's key pacemakers, with a role in many biological rhythms, including infradian rhythms. Male hamsters, for instance, show an annual rhythm in release of the hormone testosterone, which correlates with their breeding cycle. This release seems to depend on day length, increasing as days become longer and decreasing as they shorten. Damage to the SCN eliminates this annual rhythm of testosterone release and the annual breeding cycle that depends upon it.

The SCN–pineal system in birds

In birds the system is simpler, but it operates according to the same principles as in mammals. The pineal gland in birds is close to the surface of the skull, and can respond directly to light penetrating the skull bone. In this way light in the outside world can influence the release of melatonin from the pineal.

Other endogenous pacemakers

Although the SCN–pineal system is clearly a major endogenous pacemaker, there is a vast range of biological rhythms that affect behaviour and a large number of physiological processes such as hormone release. It is unlikely that the SCN–pineal system looks after all of these; in fact it has been shown that damage to the SCN does not affect the daily activity rhythm associated with the anticipation of mealtimes in rats (Rosenwasser *et al.* 1981). This activity rhythm must, therefore, be controlled by another endogenous pacemaker.

While some endogenous pacemakers or body clocks clearly respond to zeitgebers such as light, this interaction may be less important for some biological rhythms. The human female menstrual cycle, for instance, has a normal cycle length of 28 days and does not vary over the year. So this infradian rhythm seems to rely completely on endogenous pacemakers, and rarely interacts with external zeitgebers.

Issues, debates and approaches (IDA)

- *Nature/nurture debate* – Biological clocks are innate mechanisms with a clear genetic component, which emphasizes nature over nurture; it is difficult for us to change our sleep/waking patterns.

- *Reductionist explanation* – Explanations of biological rhythms are also **reductionist** as they explain them at the lowest level of physiological mechanisms, sometimes underestimating the contribution of higher-level factors such as social zeitgebers.

Examiners' notes

Throughout this section, and for most areas in psychology, research evidence is the most effective source of AO2/3 marks. Make sure you have one or two studies available to illustrate and support your understanding of the functions of the SCN and the role of melatonin.

Examiners' notes

General commentary on evidence for the existence of more than one biological clock, or on the fact that some biological rhythms rely less on external zeitgebers, can be made relevant to questions on the control of circadian rhythms. This would earn AO2/3 marks.

Research into biological rhythms

Most of the research outlined so far has been done on non-human animals and some of it has involved lesioning the brain, deliberately damaging the SCN and associated pathways. Although we can be fairly sure that human brain pacemakers such as the SCN and the pineal gland must operate in a similar way (as the pathways and structures are the same), any generalizations from animals to humans must always be made with caution. More convincing is evidence involving human participants.

Research into endogenous pacemakers

For ethical reasons we cannot do lesion studies in humans, but there are other methods we can use to investigate the interaction between endogenous pacemakers and exogenous zeitgebers in circadian rhythms. You may recall that the evening primrose and hibernating mammals maintain their biological rhythms even when kept in constant light and temperature. These are referred to as **free-running studies**, as biological rhythms are allowed to run free in the absence of the usual external zeitgebers (especially light) that synchronize the endogenous pacemaker with the outside world. Similar studies have been done in humans.

Siffre (1975)

Michel Siffre spent 179 days in a deep cave in Texas. There was no natural light. He could ask the researchers above ground for the artificial lights to be turned off when he wanted to sleep, and turned on when he woke up. They also monitored various physiological functions such as heart rate, blood pressure and body temperature.

Examiners' notes

Studies such as Siffre's are central to supporting models of the interaction between biological clocks and zeitgebers. Make sure you can provide key procedural details that help the examiner understand the findings, but focus on findings and especially conclusions.

In this strange setting, Siffre's circadian sleep/waking cycle was erratic, but eventually settled down to between 25 and 32 hours. This made his days slightly longer than normal, so that when he emerged from the cave on the 179th day, to him it was only the 151st day. Another key finding was that his body temperature circadian rhythm also extended, but remained more stable and slightly shorter than his sleep/waking cycle, at 25 hours.

Conclusions from the Siffre study

This case study of free-running circadian rhythms confirms several features of endogenous pacemakers.

- The human endogenous pacemaker tends to run a little slower than 24 hours, and needs to be synchronized each day through exogenous zeitgebers.
- The main zeitgeber in this study was light, and results confirm that light is a key zeitgeber in maintaining the synchronization between endogenous pacemakers and the outside world.
- The sleep/waking cycle and the circadian rhythm of body temperature became desynchronized. This implies that they have separate endogenous pacemakers.

Evaluation of free-running studies

The Siffre study was an extremely unusual single case study. A strength of it is the extended length that allowed Siffre's rhythms to settle into a natural free-running pattern. Even so, it is hard to assess how other factors in the cave might have influenced the sleep/wake cycle, e.g. temperature, lack of social interaction. Also, although the results of the Siffre study were fascinating, this is a single case study and conclusions based on that alone would not be reliable.

From the early 1960s to the 1980s, Aschoff and Wever (1981) carried out a series of free-running studies similar to Siffre's, using student participants housed in a specially adapted, soundproof, underground bunker, although for a much shorter timespan (three to four weeks). Their results matched Siffre's: although there were individual differences in the 300 or so participants, sleep/waking cycles in the absence of external zeitgebers extended to between 25 and 27 hours. Combining the studies provides a more reliable picture of what happens in free-running studies.

Conclusions from research into endogenous pacemakers

- Animal research has confirmed the role of endogenous pacemakers in the control of circadian rhythms.

- Studies have also demonstrated how pacemakers interact with light in their control of sleep and waking.

- The same structures and pathways exist in humans and we can assume they operate in the same way.

- Free-running studies in humans confirm that, in the absence of the zeitgeber light, our circadian sleep/waking cycle is maintained by the endogenous pacemaker, but becomes slightly desynchronized from the outside world.

Research into external zeitgebers

Most research in this area has focused on light as the external zeitgeber that is most important in the synchronization of endogenous pacemakers with the outside world. However, there are other important factors.

Artificial lighting and modern sleeping habits

Today, sleeping habits in advanced societies are not determined by darkness. We do not normally go to bed at dusk (especially in the winter when, in the UK, dusk can come mid-afternoon). Before the invention of electric light in the late 19th century, sleep/waking for the majority of people would have been determined by light and darkness. Changes in the range of zeitgebers have been relatively recent in human social evolution.

Work and social habits

In some societies it is not possible to use light and dark as zeitgebers. The Inuit in Greenland have periods in the year of 24 hours of light or 24 hours of darkness. Yet they maintain normal 24-hour sleep/waking cycles. For them, social and work habits, rather than light, are used to synchronize the sleep/waking endogenous pacemaker with the outside world.

Examiners' notes

Always try to show how the findings of different research studies support or contradict each other. This is an important aspect of How Science Works (AO3). Evaluating the methodology of single studies is effective only if you make it explicit what the implications are for the validity of findings.

Examiners' notes

Commenting on the range of zeitgebers that can interact in the control of circadian rhythms can help show your understanding of biological clocks and zeitgebers. The key to good marks is to use what you know to demonstrate this understanding.

Disruption of biological rhythms: jet lag

Light is a key zeitgeber that helps to synchronize biological clocks with the outside world. But even in the UK day length varies over the year, and this causes slight variations in our biological rhythms. However, the changes in day length are so gradual that we do not normally notice these variations. Nowadays, however, modern societies have devised a number of ways in which our biological rhythms are exposed to large and rapid changes in exogenous zeitgebers.

Understanding jet lag

For example, intercontinental plane travel has become widespread since the Second World War, so that we can move relatively rapidly between time zones. The clock time at any one point depends on the rotation of the earth over 24 hours and its position relative to the sun. For instance:

- When it is 12 noon in London, the clock time is five hours earlier in New York (i.e. 7 a.m.).
- When the sun sets at 8 p.m. in London, it is 3 p.m. in New York.

If you take a flight from London to New York, leaving at noon (midday) UK time and taking about 7 hours, you arrive at 7 p.m. UK time, but it will be only 2 p.m. local New York time. Four hours later, your biological clock, still on UK time, is preparing the body for sleep, but local cues are telling the body it is only early evening. Your biological clock has, therefore, become desynchronized from external zeitgebers.

This is what we mean by disruption of biological rhythms, and the effects of this particular type of disruption are known as **jet lag**.

Symptoms of jet lag

It became apparent early on in the age of jet travel that a significant number of passengers experienced symptoms after travel that could last a few hours or even days, before these gradually wore off. These symptoms could include:

- tiredness
- problems with attention and concentration
- irritability
- anxiety.

It also became clear that jet lag symptoms were often worse when travelling from West to East than when travelling from East to West.

Explanations for jet lag

The symptoms of jet lag can be explained through our knowledge of the interaction between endogenous pacemakers and exogenous zeitgebers, especially light.

East to West travel: phase delay

Going back to the earlier example of travelling from London to New York, we can see what happens to this interaction. In London at noon, our biological clock is synchronized with the time of day. Seven hours later, after landing land in New York, our biological clock tells our body it is 7 p.m. in the evening, but it is actually only 2 p.m. in New York. This dislocation is responsible for the symptoms of jet lag – physiological systems (such as body temperature and the sleep/waking cycle) are desynchronized from external zeitgebers (light and social cues such as mealtimes).

In this situation, with the biological clock ahead of local time, it has to 'wait' for external cues to catch up; this is known as '**phase delay**'.

West to East travel: phase advance

When we travel West to East, the desynchronization of the biological clock from external cues happens in a similar way. We leave New York at noon, and land in London seven hours later, so our body clock thinks it is 7 p.m. In fact, given the time difference, it is actually midnight local time and most people will either be in bed or preparing for sleep. The biological clock is behind local time and not ready for sleep yet – in a simple sense, it has to 'catch up' by moving forward. This is known as '**phase advance**'.

From anecdotal observations, it seems that phase advance is more difficult to adjust to than phase delay, as jet lag symptoms are worse travelling from West to East than from East to West.

North–South travel?

Note that because of the Earth's rotation, points on the same North–South line are in the same time zone. This means that jet travel from North to South (or vice versa) does not lead to the symptoms of jet lag.

Resynchronization

As outlined on pp. 8–9, one of our main biological clocks, the SCN, is directly influenced by light entering the eye, allowing it to coordinate biological rhythms with the time of day. Even with the radical desynchronization produced by jet travel, the SCN will gradually adjust to the changed time of day in its new environment. However, this takes time and the symptoms of jet lag caused by the desynchronization can often last for several days, although there are significant individual differences.

Examiners' notes

Providing this level of detail of why disruption of rhythms causes unpleasant effects clearly demonstrates your understanding of the mechanisms involved, and will earn good AO1 marks.

Research into jet lag

We can explain symptoms of jet lag using our knowledge of endogenous pacemakers and exogenous zeitgebers. However, many observations are anecdotal, especially as increasing numbers of people have their own individual experiences of jet lag to refer to. What scientific evidence is there that jet travel and shifting time zones can have serious effects on people?

Studies of occasional travellers

Recht *et al.* (1995) found that, over a three-year period, American baseball teams won 37 per cent of games when travelling from West to East (phase advance), and 44 per cent after travelling from East to West (phase delay). The difference in games won was statistically significant, and Recht and colleagues concluded that jet lag affected the players' performance and that the effects were worse after phase advance than after phase delay, as predicted.

A problem with this study is that there are many uncontrolled variables, such as:

- the relative ability of the different teams
- fluctuations in form
- the effects of injury to individual players.

We would expect the effect of these variables to even out over the three years of the study but, even so, this is not a study with high validity.

Other studies have, however, supported the conclusions. For instance, it was shown that American servicemen took on average about three days to recover from the symptoms of jet lag after travelling from Europe to the USA (East to West, phase delay), and on average eight days when travelling from the USA to Europe (West to East, phase advance).

Studies of cabin crew

A different approach is to look at people regularly exposed to jet travel. Studies of cabin crew have found that they have raised levels of stress hormones and do less well on memory tests than control participants (Cho *et al.* 2000). More dramatically, female cabin crew with years of exposure to long-haul jet travel were found to have similar symptoms, and also showed some shrinkage of brain structures in the temporal lobe (Cho 2001).

In a review of over 500 articles on aviation and health, Waterhouse *et al.* (2007) found that disrupted sleep and hormone patterns led to cabin crew experiencing decreased cognitive performance and mental health problems, including brief episodes of psychosis (loss of contact with reality), while female cabin crew complained of menstrual cycle problems.

These research studies confirm that jet travel can lead to problems with cognitive processes such as memory, and directly affect brain function and physiological processes such as our stress system.

Essential notes

The USA spans several time zones that have to be crossed when travelling East–West or West–East. New York, in the East, is five hours ahead of Anchorage in Alaska in the West.

Examiners' notes

If you use research studies as support for the effects of disruption of biological rhythms, then focus on the findings. If you use methodological evaluation of single studies, show how it makes the study unreliable (as with the Recht *et al.* study). But it is even more impressive if you can combine the findings of two or more studies to provide a general picture.

Essential notes

The studies described here are **correlational**, so we cannot directly assume a cause and effect between jet travel and symptoms. However, the accumulation of evidence and our knowledge of biological rhythms combine to produce a convincing picture.

Factors affecting severity of jet lag

As well as the direction of travel and number of time zones crossed, other factors seem to affect the severity of symptoms of jet lag.

Individual differences

Individual differences in biological rhythms make some people more or less sensitive to jet lag (Arendt 2008). This may be related to genetic influences, such as the circadian clock gene, PERIOD3 (see p. 7). This gene comes in different forms and each form seems to produce a slightly different circadian pattern.

Age

Age also seems to affect our sensitivity to jet lag, although studies are inconsistent. Some find that the effects of jet lag decrease with age (Sack *et al.* 2007), while others find the opposite (Moline *et al.* 1992).

Coping with jet lag

A great deal of research has investigated coping strategies for jet lag (reviewed in Arendt 2009), using what we know of biological clocks and exogenous zeitgebers. Key methods include the use of bright light and taking melatonin tablets.

Use of melatonin

Melatonin plays a crucial role in the SCN–pineal system that controls biological rhythms (see p. 8). It has been shown that melatonin can reduce the effects of jet lag (Takahashi *et al.* 2002). However, it is not straightforward to use, as its effects vary depending on where in the circadian cycle it is given and whether the jet lag symptoms are due to phase advance or phase delay.

Exposure to bright light

Similarly, exposure to bright light can shift circadian rhythms if used at the appropriate points in the circadian cycle; again, this has to be calculated carefully to ensure that rhythms are shifted in the right direction.

Adapting to local zeitgebers

Probably the most reliable method for reducing the symptoms of jet lag is to adapt immediately to local zeitgebers such as time of day and mealtimes. This may require use of mild stimulants such as caffeine to stay awake when the biological clock is trying to impose sleep, and going out into sunlight early in the morning. As we have seen, light is the key zeitgeber in the synchronization of circadian rhythms.

Issues, debates and approaches (IDA)

- *Real-life applications* – This is an excellent area for application of research findings to the real world. Our knowledge of the interaction between biological clocks and the zeitgeber light can be used to devise methods to reduce the effects of jet lag.

Examiners' notes

Don't forget that relevant commentary on factors affecting jet lag can be an effective source of AO1 or, especially, AO2/3 marks.

Examiners' notes

Treatments for jet lag are not on the specification. However, if you can show that the effectiveness of treatments can be explained in terms of our understanding of biological clocks and zeitgebers, then reference to treatments can earn marks.

Essential notes

Our knowledge of biological rhythms enables us to understand why jet travel produces the symptoms of jet lag. It also suggests treatments, but the fact that these are not yet consistently successful shows how complex the interaction between biological clocks and exogenous zeitgebers must be.

Disruption of biological rhythms: shift work

Shift work involves a disruption to our biological rhythms, as it requires us to be active while our biological clock is trying to impose sleep on the body. Everyone experiences this at some time: all-night parties and panic-driven revision late into the night both involve being alert and active at times when we should be sleeping. However, parties and revision only go on for a limited time and we generally recover from them quickly. Symptoms are likely to be limited to daytime tiredness.

The development of shift work

The invention of electric light at the end of the 19th century transformed not only domestic and social life, but work life too. It became possible for factories and hospitals to function for 24 hours a day, while working and socializing into the late evening became commonplace. However, while electric light enabled 24-hour working, it still required people to do the work, and this meant that some of these people had to work at unsociable times.

To spread the burden fairly between everyone, it became accepted practice for employees to alternate work periods, taking turns to work the unsociable periods. In this way, shift work became a routine feature of 24-hour occupations. These included factories and other commercial industries, as well as nurses, doctors, the police and air traffic controllers.

Shift patterns

A standard shift work pattern became three eight-hour shifts: midnight to 8 a.m. (the 'graveyard shift'), 8 a.m. to 4 p.m., 4 p.m. to midnight. Typically, workers would spend one week on one shift, then rotate. For reasons lost in history, the standard pattern was to have a **backwards rotation**: midnight to 8 a.m., then a week on 4 p.m. to midnight, and finally a week on 8 a.m. to 4 p.m.

The effects of shift work

An important function of our biological clocks is to impose sleep on the brain and the body when active behaviour is impossible, i.e. during the night (in diurnal animals such as humans). As we see on pp. 20–3, sleep is not a passive state that we fall into when nothing much is happening; rather, it is a brain state imposed by a complex network of centres in the brainstem reticular formation, linked by pathways to the SCN–pineal circadian clock system.

Under normal circumstances, our circadian rhythms mean that we fall asleep after dusk and wake up when morning comes along. Melatonin, released from the pineal gland under the control of the SCN, is extremely sensitive to light, with levels falling during daylight and rising during the night-time. This rise during darkness is thought to be a key element of the

Essential notes

Many professions operate on a 24-hour basis, including all those listed on the right. Consumers, too, have come to expect 24-hour access to goods and services, with the advent of all-night supermarkets and 24-hour telephone helplines. Providing these 24-hour-services depends on people working in shifts.

Examiners' notes

Outlining the possible mechanisms underlying the effects of shift work would be an effective way of demonstrating understanding and earning AO1 marks.

sleep control network, as melatonin has direct effects on the brainstem sleep centres.

When we try to work at 2 a.m., we are going against our circadian rhythms, and in particular we are trying to maintain alertness when our biological clock and sleep centres are imposing sleep on the brain.

Shift work and real-life incidents

You probably know from your own experience how hard it can be to work well at 2 in the morning, especially if the work requires attention and concentration. It may be possible to do it for one night, but doing this for several nights in a row can make it extremely difficult to maintain high levels of attention and concentration throughout. These effects of shift work have been implicated in a number of real-life incidents that led to disastrous consequences.

For example, it is generally accepted that the nuclear disaster in Chernobyl, Russia, in 1986, and the near nuclear meltdown at Three Mile Island, Pennsylvania, in 1979, were both in part caused by shift workers failing to notice key warning signals. Both incidents occurred in the very early morning (c. 1.30 a.m. at Chernobyl; around 4 a.m. at Three Mile Island) – exactly when we would predict attention levels would be at their worst as the workers fight off the drive to sleep.

We shall look at more systematic evidence on pp. 18–19, but, given our knowledge of biological clocks and the control of circadian rhythms, this is exactly what we would predict if biological rhythms are disrupted by shift work.

Sleep deprivation and social effects of shift work

Shift work can have effects in other (albeit less dramatic) ways. Workers on night shifts have to try and sleep in the daytime. Daytime sleep is likely anyway to be interrupted by traffic and other noise and be less restorative than night-time sleep. So night-shift workers may also be suffering the effects of mild sleep deprivation, as well as trying to stay alert when the brain wants to sleep.

In addition, people who have to sleep during the day may also be missing out on everyday family and social activities.

Effects of shift work may therefore be 'confounded' with effects of sleep deprivation, and we should be cautious in drawing conclusions from research into shift work.

Examiners' notes

Dramatic real-life examples can seem very powerful but they are uncontrolled (in scientific terms), and we rarely know all the variables involved. They can suggest possible conclusions, but need to be followed up by more systematic studies. If you refer to them, point out that they are unreliable, as this will show your awareness of How Science Works, but focus on the more controlled studies.

Examiners' notes

If you describe general issues around shift work, such as problems with daytime sleep, you will only earn marks if you make them relevant to the question, e.g. by pointing out that this can complicate the interpretation of research studies.

Research into shift work

A variety of studies have clearly demonstrated the negative effects of shift work. It has been found that nurses on night shift have significantly more road accidents (Gold *et al.* 1992). Extended periods of shift work are linked to an increase in the chances of developing breast cancer or heart disease, probably through an effect on the body's immune system (Davis *et al.* 2001).

More generally, shift workers report higher levels of stress and health problems. Under these conditions, work efficiency and productivity can be affected, as well as leading to high levels of absenteeism. So, in line with the disruption caused by jet travel, shift work can affect physiological systems and cognitive processes such as attention and memory.

Unfortunately, modern Western societies are dependent upon shift work. But with our knowledge of biological rhythms and zeitgebers, can we devise methods for coping with the negative effects?

Czeisler's (1982) study of a Utah chemical plant

A Utah chemical plant brought Czeisler in to advise on their shift work patterns. These were of the traditional type, with three eight-hour shifts on a backwards rotation of one week on each shift. Workers reported feeling stressed and having problems with sleeping. There were high levels of minor health problems and absenteeism.

Forwards shift rotation

Applying his knowledge of biological rhythms, Czeisler considered an alternative to backwards shift rotation, i.e. **forwards rotation**. This means that someone moves from a morning shift (say 7 a.m. to 3 p.m.) to an evening shift (3 p.m. to 11 p.m.) and then to a night shift (11 p.m. to 7 a.m.). Every time their shift changes, they have to extend their day a bit. For example, instead of going to bed at, say, 10 p.m. in order to be up in time for an early (7 a.m.) shift, they could delay going to bed until midnight or so, when they move to the evening shift. Extending their day is not too difficult, because that is what our free-running clock would naturally like to do as it tends to run on a 25-hour cycle (see studies into endogenous pacemakers on p. 10). In other words, it is easier to keep yourself up for longer than it is to force yourself to go to bed before you are tired. With backwards rotation, the latter applies.

Czeisler's recommendations

- Czeisler recommended moving the plant to a forwards shift pattern, arguing that it would be easier for workers to adjust to their new shifts, in the same way that phase delay is easier to adjust to in jet travel than phase advance.

- He also felt that one week was not long enough for resynchronization of the biological clock with darkness/daylight; workers were in a constant state of desynchronization. He recommended an extended pattern of 21 days on each shift.

Examiners' notes

Although there are many anecdotal accounts of the effects of shift work and jet lag, make sure you support any comments by referring to research studies rather than to anecdote.

Essential notes

Systematic studies in this area are rare, as they are costly and difficult to set up. However, Charles Czeisler showed what could be achieved.

Effects of shift pattern change

The plant adopted Czeisler's recommendations, and after nine months on the new pattern, the results were assessed. Workers reported fewer health problems and lower stress levels, and absenteeism had fallen. These positive changes were reflected in increased productivity. Overall the results supported Czeisler's analysis of how the effects of disrupted biological rhythms can be reduced, if not eliminated.

Other studies of shift work

Other studies have found similar results. Moving American police officers from a backwards shift to a forwards rotation and increasing the time per shift to 18 days' rotation led to less reported stress. There was less sleeping during shifts, and a 40 per cent reduction in accidents while working (Coren 1996).

Even on a forwards shift rotation, people still have to work at times when their biological clock is trying to impose sleep. A more permanent solution would be to keep workers on the same shift, thus (in theory) allowing their biological clock to adjust perfectly to darkness/daylight, and research has shown that this approach can indeed work. Phillips *et al.* (1991) allowed Kentucky policemen to choose which of the three shifts they would like; they then stayed on these shifts, allowing plenty of time for their biological clock to synchronize with the outside world. As predicted, fewer health- and work-related problems were found among the officers.

Although this may sound an ideal solution, it does depend on finding enough people prepared to go on permanent night shift, i.e. to try and sleep in the daytime, and to miss out on family and social activities. It is therefore not an ideal or universal solution.

Disrupting biological rhythms – conclusions

Research into biological rhythms has allowed us to understand why disruption of rhythms through jet travel and shift work can have such significant effects. It can also lead to the development of methods for reducing the effects of the disruption.

This area is an excellent example of how our social, cultural and technological evolution has put an increasing strain on our inherited brain systems for controlling biological rhythms. The invention of electric light, 24-hour working and playing, and increasingly complex and demanding jobs can disrupt the normal relationship between endogenous pacemakers and exogenous zeitgebers.

Issues, debates and approaches (IDA)

- *Real-life applications* – As the studies described here show, our knowledge of the interaction between biological clocks and the zeitgeber light can be applied in real life, enabling us to devise methods to reduce the effects of shift work.

Examiners' notes

Czeisler's study is an important example of the application of our understanding of biological rhythms. Make sure you can describe clearly how this understanding helps to explain Czeisler's results.

Examiners' notes

Replication is a key feature of How Science Works. Whenever possible, try to link studies together and compare their findings; this provides a more reliable view of research in a particular area.

Examiners' notes

General commentary can earn marks, but only if it is explicitly linked to the question. Make sure it is not personal or anecdotal, but has psychological content and is relevant to the question.

The nature of sleep

Sleep in the animal kingdom

Sleep is found throughout the animal kingdom, from reptiles and birds up to rats, cats, dogs and primates such as chimpanzees and humans. Humans may spend around a third of their lives asleep. It is assumed that a behaviour that is so common must be important, as otherwise it would have disappeared during evolution. The fact that sleep persists across the animal kingdom suggests that it has **adaptive** and valuable functions. Unfortunately, as we shall see, identifying these functions has proved to be very difficult. However, our starting point for explanations of sleep is studying the nature or characteristics of sleep, as these will give us clues to its functions.

Although all animals sleep, they can show very different patterns. The donkey sleeps for three hours a day, humans for around seven-and-a-half hours, rats for ten hours and cats for 15 hours, while the opossum has 19 hours of sleep in every 24. Even aquatic mammals such as dolphins and porpoises sleep – albeit in a particularly unusual way (see p. 23). These variations can give us clues as to the functions of sleep. For instance, even at this stage we can note that small animals tend to sleep longer than large animals.

Problems in the scientific study of sleep: the sloth

The sloth is an arboreal (tree-dwelling) mammal. It is quite large, and according to the simple association mentioned above should not sleep that much. However, early studies concluded that it slept for up to 20 hours a day.

A problem with these studies was that they were observations on sloths in captivity. More recently, a study of the sloth in its natural habitat concluded that, in fact, it slept for only around six hours a day (Rattenborg *et al.* 2008). This is in line with what we would expect from its body size. In other words, the early studies were unreliable because the animals were being kept in artificial conditions. It may be that their increased sleep was due to the boredom and monotony of life in captivity.

Types of sleep

For many years it was thought that sleep was a single state in all animals. Although we may be conscious that during sleep we are restless or having vivid dreams, it took major advances in techniques for investigating the brain before the picture of a single sleep state was overturned.

The electroencephalogram

Neurons, the cells making up the brain, conduct information using electrical impulses. This was established by the end of the 19th century, but it was only in the 1920s that techniques were devised to record the brain's electrical activity systematically. Berger (1929) introduced the **electroencephalogram (EEG)**. Using a number of recording electrodes on the surface of the scalp, he could record patterns of electrical activity from the millions of neurons making up the brain.

Researchers began using the EEG to investigate sleep states soon after, but it was the systematic studies of Kleitman, Aserinsky and Dement in the 1950s that revolutionized our understanding of sleep. By then it had been established that the EEG had two basic forms:

- The desynchronized EEG had no obvious waveform or pattern (see trace 1 in Fig. 1), although it could consist of fast or slow activity.
- The synchronized EEG has a repeated waveform (e.g. trace 5 in Fig. 1), which can be defined by its frequency (number of waves per second: hertz or Hz) and its amplitude (the size of each wave).

Early studies had shown that the EEG of the awake active brain was fast and desynchronized (see trace 1 in Fig. 1). Kleitman's group (Aserinsky and Kleitman 1953) were able to show that during a night's sleep, the EEG underwent significant changes from this waking state. They identified two distinct types of sleep:

- **non-rapid eye movement sleep (NREM)**
- **rapid eye movement sleep (REM)**.

In addition, using the EEG, they described different stages of NREM and identified that during a night's sleep we alternate between REM and NREM in a highly systematic ultradian rhythm (see p. 6).

In Fig. 1, the various EEG patterns are shown, and these relate to the sleep stages described on p. 22.

Examiners' notes

NREM is sometimes referred to as slow-wave sleep (SWS). Technically, this term applies only to the last two stages of NREM, where slow delta waves are seen. However, some textbooks use the two terms, NREM and SWS, as equivalents.

REM sleep is also sometimes called desynchronized sleep.

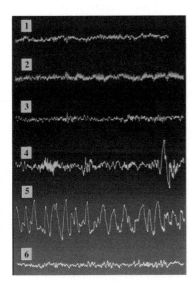

Fig. 1
EEG recording of brain waves in various states of sleep:
Trace 1: brain activity of a person when awake
Trace 2: alpha waves of a person drowsy but still awake, with eyes closed, receiving no external stimuli
Trace 3: theta waves as the person falls into stage 1 sleep
Trace 4: more complex patterns as sleep deepens, including sleep spindles characteristic of stage 2 sleep
Trace 5: standard delta-wave pattern usually associated with deep sleep (stages 3 and 4)
Trace 6: REM sleep (similar to trace 1)

This topic continues on the next spread. ☞

NREM and REM sleep

Research over the last 50 years has confirmed the original observations of Kleitman's group – that there are two distinct states of sleep, REM and NREM.

- In REM, the brain seems to have an aroused pattern, but the body muscles are paralysed.
- In NREM, the EEG is synchronized, and the deep stages are dominated by large, slow delta waves.

Stages of non-rapid eye movement sleep (NREM)

- *Stage 1:* The EEG of the drowsy person shows theta waves (small waves with a frequency of 4 to 7 Hz).
- *Stage 2:* As the person falls asleep, the EEG is still dominated by theta waves, but the amplitude of the waves increases. Sleep spindles occur, i.e. short bursts of high-frequency spikes.
- *Stage 3:* Delta waves are seen (high-amplitude slow waves (1 to 4 Hz)), and sleep spindles are less frequent.
- *Stage 4:* This is the deepest stage of NREM, with the EEG dominated by delta waves. The person is deeply asleep.

REM sleep

From falling asleep to stage 4 NREM takes around an hour. Then sleep lightens and the person moves back into stage 2 NREM. At this point, there is a shift into REM sleep, characterized in the EEG by fast desynchronized activity. Sleep is accompanied by rapid movements of the eyes (hence the name) and twitching of the extremities. Skeletal muscle tone is lost and the person is effectively paralysed.

After about 20 minutes in REM, the person slips back into stage 2 NREM, and the process repeats itself: stage 2 to stage 4 NREM, then lightening back to stage 2. The cycle of REM alternating with NREM takes about 90 minutes, so there are about four to five cycles per night.

Dreaming

Dement and Kleitman (1957) also established the close relationship between REM and dreaming. Participants woken during REM reported dreams about 80 per cent of the time. For NREM, the figure was about 20 per cent, and the dreams were less vivid and more fragmented. For many years it was acceptable to refer to REM sleep as 'dreaming sleep'. For a time it was also referred to as 'paradoxical sleep'. This was because while the person was still deeply asleep, the EEG showed the fast desynchronized pattern typical of the waking state.

Essential notes

New technology allows us to monitor sleep and waking states in ever more detail. Functional magnetic resonance imaging (fMRI) can show the location and patterning of electrical cerebral activity, for example when the sleeping brain hears an auditory stimulus. This will eventually throw light on cognitive processing ability while asleep.

Examiners' notes

Remember to tailor your answer to the marks available. An AO1 question on the nature of sleep for 4 marks requires half the material as one for 8 marks. Also decide whether you will go for breadth or depth; if the question allows, either a detailed account of the EEG stages of sleep or a less detailed account of several aspects of the nature of sleep would access the available marks.

Essential notes

We know dreaming isn't entirely confined to REM sleep but the percentages found in REM and NREM sleep are changing. The more sophisticated sleep research methods become, the more dreaming is found in NREM.

Essential notes

Sleep paralysis during REM prevents us from the potentially dangerous activity of acting out our dreams, although, in some sleep disorders such as **somnambulism** (sleepwalking), this doesn't seem to happen.

REM and NREM sleep across the animal kingdom

It is now established that the two stages of sleep and the alternating pattern between REM and NREM are found throughout the animal kingdom, showing that they have a long evolutionary history. Details vary between species, but this consistency is impressive. There are one or two exceptions.

Dolphins and porpoises
Aquatic mammals such as dolphins and porpoises do not seem to have REM sleep but only NREM. Even more strangely, they show NREM only on one side of the brain, while the other shows an aroused EEG pattern. However this begins to make sense when we consider the dolphin's ecological niche or habitat. Aquatic mammals have to come to the surface to breathe, and also have to be alert for predators and debris in the water around them. A stage of complete deep sleep could be fatal for them.

Even before EEG recordings were made, it was noted (Lilly 1964) that dolphins slept with one eye open! Research then found that the open eye was controlled by the aroused hemisphere. So, in order to stay alert all the time, the dolphin and other aquatic mammals sleep with one hemisphere of the brain at a time, while the other hemisphere is actively controlling vision through the eye it controls. The evolution of such a complicated arrangement for dolphin sleep is strong evidence that sleep must have important functions.

Migrating birds
Researchers have shown that some birds can sleep unihemispherically, both on the ground and (to a lesser extent) during long hours of migratory flight. When one hemisphere is asleep, the eye connected to the alert hemisphere remains open, which keeps the bird semi-alert to danger. Rattenborg (2006) has suggested that this is only possible for NREM sleep, which can occur in one or both cerebral hemispheres, rather than for REM sleep, which always occurs in both hemispheres, because the muscle paralysis which accompanies REM sleep is not compatible with flight.

Modern sleep research

Today, scientific research into sleep takes place in the sleep laboratory using **polysomnography**. This term refers to the simultaneous recording of many different physiological measures. These include the EEG, eye movements, heart rate, levels of hormones in the blood stream and muscle activity. These, plus videoing of the participant during the night, provide a comprehensive picture of bodily changes during sleep.

Although this makes sleep study very scientific we have to remember that the sleep laboratory is a very artificial environment. Sleep patterns may not represent sleep in the participant's home setting. Most studies therefore only begin recording after the participant has had at least one night's sleep to familiarize themselves with the laboratory setting.

Essential notes

Cross-species comparisons are useful when trying to find out what sleep is for, but conclusions must be made with caution because of many other variables such as life style, habitat and whether an animal is nocturnal or not.

Lifespan changes in sleep

Individual differences in sleep

Major changes take place in the amount and patterning of sleep over the human lifespan, and these may provide clues to the functions of sleep.

It is also important to remember that individuals vary greatly in how much sleep they need, or can get by on. There are people who function efficiently on four to five hours a night, and others who seem to need nine to ten hours per night. The average in humans is about 7.5 hours.

Age-related changes

At birth, babies sleep for around 15 hours a day, but – more remarkably – 50 per cent of this is REM sleep (see Fig. 2). By the age of 2, the adult pattern of around eight hours sleep a night (though still supplemented by daytime naps) has emerged, with 20 to 25 per cent REM. These changes early in life are probably the most dramatic of the lifespan changes in sleep, but reviews (Ohayon *et al.* 2004) have identified gradual variations that occur over the rest of the lifespan:

- Deep NREM (stages 3 and 4) decreases from about 24 per cent of total sleep time at age 5 to only 9 per cent at age 70.
- REM decreases less dramatically, from 25 per cent of total sleep time at age 5 to 19 per cent at age 70.
- There are slight increases in stages 1 and 2 NREM.
- There is a decrease in total sleep time from about 8 hours at age 5 to about 6 hours at age 70.

Essential notes

Don't forget that you can use material wherever it is relevant. Several aspects of lifespan changes in sleep are relevant to explanations for the functions of sleep, in particular the large amount of sleep in the newborn – think how this might relate to restoration and maintenance of brain circuits (see p. 28).

Fig. 2
Changes in proportions of NREM and REM sleep with age

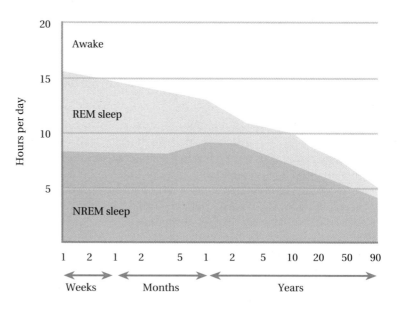

Adolescent sleep patterns

Another interesting aspect of the study of sleep across the lifespan is sleep in adolescence. Adolescence is a time of major change within the brain, involving reorganization of neural pathways and synapses. Alongside this, there are major changes in daily activities, with social life, school work, TV and social networking taking up an increasing amount of time. There is evidence that this shifts sleep patterns, with adolescents sleeping less in the week and more at weekends, and sleeping less overall than other adults. On this basis, it has even been suggested that the school day should start later to allow the adolescent to catch up on sleep loss (Wolfson and Carskadon 2005). If REM and deep NREM are associated with brain growth and development, then this suggestion is not as outrageous as it may sound.

Implications of lifespan changes in sleep

What might explain the high proportion of REM in the newborn? This is a time of rapid brain growth, especially new synaptic connections between neurons. It is also a time when large amounts of information are being processed, and the baby is experiencing and learning new things all the time. As time passes, the rate of brain growth slows as does the pace of learning. So, if the amount of REM is related to brain growth and learning, then it would decrease as these decrease. This is supported by the continual decline of REM into old age, when brain growth has stopped and there is less learning of new material.

The lifespan reduction in deep NREM is less easy to explain. We shall see later that stages 3 and 4 NREM (along with REM) have been linked to brain restoration and are especially important for cognitive processes such as memory and attention. It may be that a gradual loss of these stages is a natural ageing process and could explain the decline in cognitive abilities that we see in old age.

Conclusions

- We can identify general changes in sleep patterns over the lifespan, and some of these, such as the high proportion of REM in the newborn, are valuable clues as to the functions of the different types of sleep.

- It should also be remembered that there are significant individual differences in sleep patterns. We cannot explain, for instance, why some adults need only five hours sleep a night and others need nine hours.

- Sleep patterns can also be affected by outside factors. As we saw with adolescents, daily activities can interfere with sleep. Other factors include medical conditions and treatments for them. It has also been suggested that disrupted sleep patterns in the elderly are often associated with illness and medications (Vitiello 2006), so scientific research into sleep patterns has to be careful to control for these outside factors.

Functions of sleep: evolutionary explanations

We have already seen that sleep is found throughout the animal kingdom, and that we can usually identify both REM and NREM components. This suggests that sleep has important functions for all animals. It is a basic principle of evolution that behaviours that are not adaptive in some way are 'selected out' during evolution, so if sleep was not important it should have disappeared. For example, the dolphin's bizarre sleep pattern has evolved to make sure that it is constantly alert in its aquatic environment; it could easily have been selected out if sleep was not so important.

Although sleep is found in all animals, the patterns vary a great deal:
- Some animals are **nocturnal**, sleeping in the daytime and active at night.
- Others are **diurnal**, sleeping at night and awake in the daytime.

Amounts of sleep, and amounts of REM and NREM, are extremely variable across different species. These observations have led to several explanations.

Webb's (1974) hibernation theory

The evolutionary approach states that sleep is adaptive. Webb proposes that an important adaptation is that sleep conserves energy, using the analogy of winter hibernation in animals such as bears. Nocturnal animals cannot be active in daytime, and diurnal animals are not suited to be active at night. Sleeping when they cannot be active saves energy – even though REM sleep is quite an active state, we know that overall we do save energy when we are asleep.

Evaluation of Webb's theory
- *Availability of food* – In support of Webb's explanation is the observation that animals sleep more when food is scarce (Berger and Phillips 1995), presumably conserving more energy.
- *Basal metabolic rate* – Webb's theory is also supported by the fact that, in general, small animals sleep more than larger animals. Small animals have a relatively high basal metabolic rate (BMR), which is the rate at which they burn up energy. If sleep helps to conserve energy, it would make sense for them to sleep more than larger animals with lower BMRs.

Meddis (1975) and safety from predation

In its simplest form, this explanation proposes that animals sleep in order to keep safe from predation when active behaviour is impossible. However, the amount of sleep would vary with several other factors. For instance:
- Herbivores that have to graze for many hours simply have less time to sleep than carnivores, which tend to have occasional but large meals.
- In addition, animals with a safe place to sleep, such as shrews in their burrow or bats high up in caves, can sleep in safety compared with animals such as zebras and antelopes, which sleep on the open savannah.

Evaluation of Meddis's theory

- *Isn't sleep more risky than quiet alertness?* – Because it includes lifestyle factors, Meddis's theory can be called an ecological account of sleep. One obvious limitation is that, if safety from predation was the key element, then in fact it makes more sense for an animal to remain quiet but alert to be completely safe.

- *Why REM and NREM?* – Meddis's theory also fails to explain why animals have two different types of sleep, REM and NREM.

- *Supportive research* – In support of Meddis, research shows the importance of ecological factors in sleeping patterns. A number of studies (Allison and Cicchetti 1976; Lesku *et al.* 2006) have looked at sleep patterns across more than 50 species and identified some important correlations:
  - Predators have more total sleep time (TST) than animals preyed upon.
  - Carnivores sleep for longer than herbivores.
  - Animals with safe sleeping sites such as burrows have more sleep and, in particular, more REM sleep than animals with dangerous sleep sites.

- *Correlational research* – Supportive findings show that ecological factors emphasized by Meddis are important in determining sleeping patterns. However, it should be emphasized that much of this research is **correlational**, meaning that we cannot draw conclusions about cause and effect. More importantly, it can be hard to disentangle the relationships between the various factors. For instance, predators are by definition carnivores (although not all carnivores are predators), so it may be that predators sleep more because they are carnivores rather than because they are predators. Similarly, small animals tend to have safer sleeping sites (zebras would find it hard to dig out a safe burrow). Since small animals sleep for longer than large animals to conserve energy, it might be this – rather than the safe sleep site – that leads to longer sleep times.

- *Multiple evolutionary causes* – It is more likely that sleep patterns involve an interaction between several of these evolutionary/ecological factors. This means that the evolutionary/ecological approach is not reductionist, as it takes a high-level, complex view of sleep and does not reduce it to one or two simple factors. However, although it has identified some separate correlations between ecological factors and the different types of sleep, it still has no clear model of why animals have evolved both REM and NREM sleep.

Issues, debates and approaches (IDA)

- *Not reductionist* – Evolutionary accounts are not reductionist (unlike restoration theories, see p. 29), but they focus on high-level ecological factors and put little emphasis on physiological processes.

- *Methodological issues* – The evolutionary approach often involves observational studies, with little control over extraneous variables but high ecological validity.

Essential notes

Don't forget that research that supports a theory can always be used as a positive evaluation point for any topic.

Examiners' notes

Commentary that discusses the problem of trying to separate out the influence of evolutionary/ecological factors is a relevant and valuable source of AO2/3 marks. It also shows that you understand the limitations of correlational studies.

Examiners' notes

Examiners are aware that IDA may be less available in some areas. For instance, in relation to sleep, gender differences in the nature of sleep and in lifespan changes are largely ignored.

Functions of sleep: restoration explanations

It has long been assumed that sleep is for restoration. When we go without sleep we feel tired and function less effectively. Therefore, we sleep to prevent these feelings of tiredness and fatigue, and to restore physiological systems that have been active in the day.

In this sense, sleep has a homeostatic function. **Homeostasis** refers to the maintenance of a constant internal environment, so sleep contributes to this by restoring physiological systems to their optimal level.

Oswald (1980)

Oswald initially observed that patients who were recovering from brain damage spent more time in REM sleep. He also noted that in the deep stages of NREM, there was a surge of growth hormone release. Growth hormone is essential for the maintenance and repair of the body's physiological systems. On the basis of these and other observations, Oswald proposed that REM sleep was a time for restoration of brain systems, while NREM was a time for restoration of the body's physiological systems.

Horne (1988)

This theory is based on a large number of laboratory-based sleep deprivation studies. These studies assume that assessing the effects of *not* sleeping will help us understand the normal functions of sleep. Horne reviewed over 50 such studies and reached the following conclusions.

- Mild sleep deprivation had little or no effect – even severe deprivation over several nights did not have dramatic consequences.
- What effects there were concentrated on cognitive functions such as attention, perception and memory.
- When deprived participants were allowed to sleep, they recovered far more of the REM and deep NREM sleep they had lost than the lighter stages of NREM.

Using this evidence, Horne proposed that REM and deep NREM (which together he called 'core sleep') were essential for maintaining those brain systems that underlie cognitive processes. Light NREM had no key function, and Horne called it 'optional sleep'. He suggested that sleep was not related to bodily restoration, which took place during 'relaxed wakefulness'.

Evaluation of restoration explanations of sleep

Animal deprivation studies

Severe sleep deprivation in rats leads to death (Everson *et al.* 1989; Rechstaffen *et al.* 1983), supporting a restoration explanation of the functions of sleep. However, keeping rats awake involves constant arousal and stress (e.g. they fall into water if they fall asleep), and it may be the stress that is fatal. A general effect of stress is supported by the fact that no single cause of death in these rats has been found.

Fatal familial insomnia
Fatal familial insomnia (FFI) is a rare inherited condition. Those humans affected sleep normally until middle age, but then simply stop sleeping, and death usually occurs within two years. Although this seems to parallel the severe deprivation studies in rats, FFI is linked to damage to the **thalamus** in the brain. It is likely that death may be caused by the damage to the thalamus rather than just by sleep deprivation.

Energy expenditure
If Oswald is correct, then expending physical energy should lead to extended sleep the following night as the body restores physiological processes. However, although findings are not entirely consistent, there is evidence that exercise causes people to fall asleep faster, but they do not sleep for longer (Breedlove *et al.* 2007). This would not support Oswald.

Growth hormone
Oswald first noted a surge of growth hormone during NREM sleep, linking this to restoration of body tissues during REM. However, Horne points out that, for growth hormone to promote protein synthesis (and therefore tissue restoration), there needs to be a supply of amino acids, the building blocks of proteins. Amino acids are part of our diet, but they are only available for protein synthesis for a few hours after eating. By the time we sleep, levels of amino acids are low and it is unlikely that much tissue restoration could take place regardless of the surge of growth hormone.

Laboratory studies of sleep deprivation
These studies, under carefully controlled conditions, provide the best evidence on the effects of sleep deprivation. Horne's analysis of these studies demonstrated that deprivation seems to affect the brain and cognitive functions rather than the body, supporting his explanation that core sleep is for brain restoration.

Restoration and evolutionary explanations
Restoration and evolutionary explanations of the functions of sleep are not necessarily alternatives. Sleep may be important for the maintenance of brain function, but the actual timing and patterning of sleep may depend on the range of evolutionary and ecological factors discussed on pp. 26–7.

Issues, debates and approaches (IDA)

- *Reductionist* – Restoration explanations are reductionist in that they emphasize low-level physiological processes. They also ignore the ecological variables that we know influence sleep patterns.

- *Methodological issues* – Restoration explanations can involve laboratory-based studies of sleep deprivation in humans, with high levels of control but low ecological validity.

- *Ethical issues* – The restoration approach can involve laboratory studies of sleep deprivation using non-human animals. The methods used are unethical and highly stressful, which also makes the findings unreliable.

Examiners' notes
If a question requires you to focus on either evolutionary or restoration explanations of the functions of sleep, remember that you can use the alternative approach as AO2/3 material. Don't provide too much detail of the alternative, but emphasize the existence of alternative approaches and briefly mention supporting evidence.

Insomnia

Insomnia is a **dyssomnia**, which is the overall term used to refer to any disturbance or difficulty related to sleep, including problems falling asleep or staying asleep, as seen in insomnia, or disorders leading to excessive daytime sleepiness, such as **sleep apnoea** or **narcolepsy**.

Insomnia can be defined as problems with sleep patterns and, in particular, difficulties in falling asleep or maintaining sleep. If it occurs regularly or over a long period of time, it is called chronic insomnia. Key features of insomnia include:

- **sleep onset latency** (time taken to fall asleep) of more than 30 minutes
- **sleep efficiency** (time in bed actually asleep) of less than 85 per cent
- several night-time awakenings.

All types of insomnia can lead to daytime drowsiness, poor concentration and the inability to feel refreshed and rested in the morning.

Polysomnography

The scientific study of sleep began in fairly primitive laboratories in the 1950s. Nowadays sleep laboratories are highly sophisticated. During a night's sleep a variety of measures can be taken, including brain activity, eye movements, body and limb movements, heart rate, blood pressure and levels of oxygen circulating in the blood. The use of these multiple measures is known as polysomnography, which enables the researcher to obtain a full picture of all the physiological and behavioural events happening in sleep.

Categories of insomnia

Insomnia is divided into two categories:

- **Primary insomnia** occurs in the absence of any obvious precipitating cause.
- **Secondary insomnia** is associated with a clear precipitating cause, such as a medical condition or psychological disorder.

Explanations for primary insomnia

A problem with explaining primary insomnia is the very fact that there is no clear precipitating factor. Two possible explanations are the genetic explanation and the hyperarousal explanation.

Genetic explanation

The control of sleep involves a highly sophisticated network of biological clocks and brainstem sleep mechanisms (see pp. 6–9 and 20–9). Much of this system is innate, and an inherited minor imbalance in this system could lead to primary insomnia. In support of this is the fact that some forms of primary insomnia begin very early in life, and that there is evidence from family studies for a genetic component in primary insomnia (Riemann *et al.* 2010).

Hyperarousal explanation

A more popular explanation links primary insomnia to a state of chronic (long-lasting) physiological arousal. It has been shown that various measures, such as heart rate and levels of stress hormones such as cortisol, are increased in people with primary insomnia. They also show high levels of anxiety, which itself involves increased arousal (Riemann *et al.* 2010).

A tendency to chronic arousal is then maintained by high arousal and anxiety about not being able to sleep.

Although a popular explanation for primary insomnia, a problem for the hyperarousal approach is that research findings are not entirely consistent. Some studies find no difference in measures of arousal between those with primary insomnia and controls. So although the weight of evidence supports a role for hyperarousal, it is not yet a complete explanation (Riemann *et al.* 2010).

Explanations for secondary insomnia

Conditions causing insomnia

There is no doubt that insomnia can be secondary to a number of conditions. These include:

- medical conditions – such as asthma, Parkinson's disease and heart failure
- psychological disorders – such as depression, anxiety, obsessive-compulsive disorder (OCD) and post-traumatic stress disorder (PTSD)
- overuse of stimulants – such as caffeine, alcohol and nicotine
- parasomnias – events that disrupt sleep but may not lead to daytime sleepiness; examples include **restless legs syndrome** and sleep apnoea, in which breathing stops for brief periods.

Other factors

Once established, secondary insomnia may also be maintained by the factors above. Other factors have also been shown to affect insomnia:

- *Genetics* – Twin studies have shown that there is a significant genetic component in insomnia (Watson *et al.* 2006). This genetic vulnerability makes it more likely that someone will develop insomnia in response to the conditions outlined above.
- *Personality* – There is evidence that people with high levels of neuroticism are more vulnerable to insomnia (Heath *et al.* 1998). Neuroticism is a personality trait associated with increased levels of anxiety and arousal.
- *Gender* – More women than men are diagnosed with insomnia, both primary and secondary (Morin *et al.* 1999). This has not been researched to any great extent, but it may be related to the fact that women have been found to have higher levels of neuroticism and anxiety than men (Lynn and Martin 1997).

Secondary insomnia would appear to be relatively straightforward to explain – and hence to treat. However, the position is not that simple, as explained on pp. 32–33.

Examiners' notes

Where possible, use research findings and conclusions to evaluate explanations, and do not be afraid to point out inconsistencies in the research evidence; this is How Science Works. Unless the question specifically requires you to evaluate studies, only do this if it can be explicitly linked to the validity of the findings or is relevant to issues and debates.

Examiners' notes

There is some debate over whether alcohol and nicotine are both stimulants and depressants. It is argued that both are stimulants at first and then become depressants as they increase in quantity. Their effects on the body are complex and also seem to be affected by context.

Issues in the diagnosis of insomnia

Diagnosing secondary insomnia

The cause of secondary insomnia is sometimes very straightforward to identify. Sleep apnoea, for instance, is easy to diagnose in the sleep laboratory. Similarly, a medical condition such as heart failure can be clearly linked to sleeping difficulties.

Treatment of the apnoea or the heart condition then helps reduce the insomnia. However, many cases of secondary insomnia are associated with psychological conditions such as anxiety and, especially, depression.

Identifying causal pathways in depression and insomnia

To show that insomnia is secondary to depression, certain conditions have to be satisfied. For instance:

- The depression has to precede the insomnia.
- The insomnia should vary in severity as the depression varies in severity.

We rely heavily on the patient's self-report, and such reports can be unclear as to exactly how the depression and the insomnia are related. This means that we cannot be sure that the depression actually caused the insomnia. In fact it has been proposed that the chain of events can be the opposite way round – insomnia can actually lead to depression (Lichstein *et al.* 2006). There is evidence in favour of this explanation:

- As outlined on pp. 16–19, disruption of the circadian sleep/waking cycle through shift work and jet lag can often lead to insomnia, as well as to anxiety, depression and health problems. So we know that insomnia can affect psychological and physical health.
- In patients diagnosed with insomnia secondary to depression, treatments such as cognitive-behavioural therapy (CBT) targeted at the insomnia have been shown simultaneously to reduce depressive symptoms. This suggests that the insomnia, not the depression, was the primary problem (Stepanski and Rybarczyk 2006)

Researchers should not, therefore, simply accept that a patient has a secondary insomnia just because they say that they cannot sleep because of depression or anxiety. Researchers need to be sure that one or the other clearly occurred first. If not, it is now common for the conditions to be considered **comorbid**, which simply means 'occurring together'.

The role of 'learned anxiety'

A problem with understanding and treating insomnia concerns precipitating and maintaining (perpetuating) factors. Once insomnia develops, whether primary or secondary, people usually try various techniques to cope with it. These may be sensible (such as keeping regular sleep/waking habits and not staying in bed too long even if tired) or less sensible (such as overuse of alcohol or drugs). If these techniques do not work, then anxiety over sleep increases and this maintains the insomnia.

Examiners' notes

It can be difficult to identify AO2/3 material in this section. But it is possible to present factors affecting insomnia as commentary on explanations, as any explanation needs to take these other factors into account.

Additional AO2/3 can include the problems with research into insomnia, such as issues with diagnosis and treatment. General problems in sleep research can be used for evaluation of all sleep research.

This 'learned' anxiety makes treatment more difficult. Even if the main cause of the insomnia is identified and removed, the learned anxiety can maintain the condition. In some sleep disorders, CBT has proved successful in addressing these psychological factors (Stepanski and Rybarczyk 2006).

Sleep state misperception

One interesting discovery has been that patients referred to sleep clinics with either primary or secondary insomnia actually show normal sleep patterns in the sleep laboratory. This condition is known as sleep state misperception; the patient genuinely feels they sleep badly and complain of daytime sleepiness, but show normal sleep onset latencies and sleep patterns. In these cases, the problem may be psychological rather than physiological.

Problems in sleep disorders research

Ecological validity of sleep research

The use of polysomnography in a sleep laboratory means that research into sleep disorders is highly scientific. However, a risk with highly controlled studies is that the findings may lack **ecological validity** and thus not generalize well to other contexts. For example, at home, people may sleep with a partner whose presence and own sleep patterns are not replicated in a laboratory study. One solution to this is to use polysomnographic measures in an individual's normal sleeping environment as far as possible and to supplement these with video recordings.

Individual differences

In 2005, Van Dongen *et al.* summarized a number of ways in which sleep preferences differ between individuals and which are known to affect daily functioning; in other words, each one of us has an individual somnotypology. This includes:

- *Circadian preference, or* **chronotype** – This refers to an individual's stable pattern of sleep/waking. At the extremes are morning types ('larks') who wake earlier and go to sleep earlier, and evening types ('owls') who wake later but are happier going to sleep later.
- *Amount of sleep needed* – Some people can function well on four or five hours' sleep, while others need nine or ten hours.
- *Night-time waking* – Some people wake more often than others in the night and are untroubled by it, while others find it impairs their overall sleep quality.
- *Napping* – Some people regularly nap in the day, while others do not or cannot.

In the view of Van Dongen and colleagues, sleep researchers rarely take individual differences in somnotypology into account at the start of studies of sleep. This means that there could be many uncontrolled extraneous variables obscuring the effects they are looking for. They argue that researchers should begin to take individuals' somnotypology into account as a matter of routine if they are to produce results that are reliable and valid.

Examiners' notes

Awareness of changes in the scientific study of sleep is very relevant to How Science Works. A brief comment on the advantages and disadvantages of polysomnography, for instance, can earn AO2/3 marks.

Examiners' notes

Van Dongen *et al's*. recommendation that individual somnotypologies are a source of potentially uncontrolled extraneous variation can be used to query the results of any sleep study that has not explicitly taken them into account.

Narcolepsy

Explanations for narcolepsy

Narcolepsy is an unusual sleep disorder affecting around 1 in 2000 people. The symptoms are clear cut:

- *excessive daytime sleepiness* – with sufferers falling rapidly into sleep episodes of 10 to 20 minutes several times a day; these can occur regardless of the situation, e.g. in class, at mealtimes or in meetings
- *cataplexy* – a sudden loss of muscle tone leading to physical collapse even during waking hours; people with narcolepsy may have several attacks a day
- *hypnagogic hallucinations* – auditory or visual hallucinations, rather like dreams, that occur particularly when just falling asleep or just waking up
- *sleep paralysis* – an inability to move, often occurring in the period between sleeping and being fully awake

Narcolepsy and REM sleep

Polysomnography (see p. 30) reveals that, whenever they fall asleep, people with narcolepsy move directly into REM sleep, rather than moving first down and then up the stages of NREM sleep. Our knowledge of the characteristics of REM sleep enables us to explain some of the key symptoms of narcolepsy:

1. During REM sleep, muscle tone is lost and we are effectively paralysed, so moving directly into REM would lead to immediate physical collapse, i.e. cataplexy.
2. Sleep paralysis could again be due to REM sleep abnormality for the same reason.
3. Most dreams occur during REM sleep; if people with narcolepsy have problems in the control of REM sleep, hypnagogic hallucinations might be the result.

This approach explains narcolepsy through abnormalities in the control of REM sleep, with the result that REM characteristics intrude into waking life. But this explanation still leaves the problems of what causes the abnormalities in REM sleep. The first clue to this came from dogs.

Research findings: hypocretin deficiency and the autoimmune system

Some dogs have a natural tendency to develop the symptoms of narcolepsy, in particular cataplexy. Breeding these dogs together eventually produces animals extremely vulnerable to cataplexy, collapsing whenever excited.

It turned out that cataplexy in dogs was linked to a gene on chromosome 12 (Lin *et al.* 1999). This gene controls the activity of a brain neurotransmitter called **hypocretin** (also known as orexin), and narcolepsy in dogs was associated with low levels of hypocretin. It was also found that, in humans with narcolepsy, there was a drastic reduction in hypocretin-producing

Examiners' notes

For questions on explanations of sleep disorders, don't spend too long describing symptoms and characteristics, as AO1 marks will be for the description of *explanations*. Give enough detail so that you can evaluate explanations by showing how they account for the key symptoms.

Essential notes

Work on narcoleptic dogs was pioneered by the well-known sleep researcher Dement, at Stanford University in the 1970s. He bred a colony of narcoleptic dogs that eventually enabled Mignot (1999) to establish the genetic basis of narcolepsy. The findings were further supported by other researchers who were able to breed hypocretin-deficient, and hence narcoleptic, mice.

cells in the hypothalamus (Thannickal *et al.* 2000) and a corresponding lack of hypocretin in the cerebrospinal fluid where it would normally be found.

The problem still remained of what caused the loss of hypocretin neurons (brain cells). Attention shifted to another genetic factor. This gene, on chromosome 6, regulates the immune system, and is known as the HLA complex gene. Our immune system protects us from infections by viruses and bacteria. However, it can go wrong. In some conditions (known as **autoimmune diseases**), such as rheumatoid arthritis and Type 1 diabetes, the immune system fails to recognize the body's own tissues and attacks them.

Research studies then found that the majority of people with narcolepsy carried a particular form (mutation) of the HLA complex gene and also had massive reductions in hypocretin neurons in the hypothalamus (Overeem *et al.* 2008). The current view, therefore, is that mutations in the HLA complex lead to the immune system selectively attacking and destroying hypocretin neurons in the brain. Hypocretin is vital to the control of REM sleep, so the loss of hypocretin neurons leads to abnormalities of REM sleep and the symptoms of narcolepsy.

Evaluation of the autoimmune disease explanation

- *Support from human research* – Although the early research was on dogs, raising problems of generalizing to humans, subsequent research has confirmed a significant link between the HLA complex gene, hypocretin and narcolepsy. In particular, narcolepsy is associated with significant reductions in hypocretin neurons in the hypothalamus.

- *Cannot be the whole answer* – The autoimmune disease explanation for narcolepsy cannot be the whole answer. There are people with the HLA mutation who do not show the symptoms of narcolepsy, and some people with narcolepsy who do not have the HLA mutation.

- *Non-genetic factors are important* – MZ (identical) twins show a **concordance rate** of about 30 per cent for narcolepsy (Overeem *et al.* 2008). As the majority of MZ twins do not show concordance, it must mean that non-genetic psychological and environmental factors are involved. At the moment, we do not know what these non-genetic factors might be. Possible candidates include infections, diet or exposure to environmental toxins that may in some way damage hypocretin neurons.

- *Insights from drug treatments* – Raising hypocretin levels artificially should help people with narcolepsy. However, drugs to achieve this are not yet available, but will eventually be a key test of the hypocretin/narcolepsy link. Animal studies offer some hope. Siegel *et al.* (2001) increased activity levels in dogs by giving them intravenous hypocretin, and Sakurai (2007) found that hypocretin injections caused rats to stay awake for longer, but Nishino and Okuro (2010) argued that, as hypocretin given in this way cannot pass from the blood to the brain, symptoms alone were being treated rather than the cause.

Essential notes

HLA stands for Human Leukocyte Antigen.

Examiners' notes

Biological explanations can seem very complicated. Focus on the line of argument and show your understanding of the explanation. Examiners will tolerate mistakes in spellings of complex terms and do not require extensive detail of the biology involved.

Essential notes

A concordance rate of 30 per cent means that, if one twin has a condition, it will also be seen in 30 per cent of co-twins.

Examiners' notes

MZ twin studies are popular research tools for investigating behaviour. Show you understand why they are important by pointing out that MZ twins are genetically identical, so any behaviour that is entirely genetic should be shown by *both* twins, i.e. showing a concordance rate of 100 per cent.

Examiners' notes

IDA points relevant to narcolepsy include the fact that explanations are reductionist and research involving non-human animals raises ethical issues. For more about these points, see p. 37.

Sleepwalking

Sleepwalking, or **somnambulism**, is when people leave their beds while asleep and walk around as if awake. Episodes are usually quite short, from a few seconds to a few minutes. However, in this time they may carry out quite complicated activities, such as making a cup of tea. Sleepwalkers can be awoken without danger and have no recollection of what they did.

Sleepwalking is common in childhood, with maybe up to 30 per cent of 5 to12 year olds having occasional episodes. It usually disappears by adolescence, although around 3 per cent of adults still suffer from the disorder.

Psychodynamic explanations of somnambulism

An early Freudian interpretation was that sleepwalkers were acting out dreams, as their behaviour can look directed and purposeful. However, this explanation can be easily discredited. Polysomnography shows that sleepwalking takes place during the deeper stages of NREM sleep. Dreams usually occur in REM sleep. In REM, the muscles of the body are effectively paralysed and it would be impossible to act out dreams.

Biological explanations of somnambulism

Genetics
Sleepwalking tends to run in families, and twin studies have found that concordance rates are 55 per cent in MZ twins and 35 per cent in DZ (non-identical) twins. Although this supports a genetic involvement, the fact that the MZ concordance is well below 100 per cent shows that significant non-genetic psychological and environmental factors must also be involved.

Brain development
The fact that sleepwalking is more common in children and that most children grow out of it suggests that it may be due to delayed development of the complex networks controlling sleep (Oliverio 2008) This is an appealing idea, although there is no direct evidence for it. Even if it were the case, it would not account for sleepwalking in adults, or why adults are more likely to sleepwalk when stressed.

Brain arousal
Polysomnography shows that during sleepwalking episodes the EEG shows a mixture of slow delta waves, typical of deep NREM stages of sleep, and beta waves, which are more typical of the aroused waking state. This suggests that the brain is incompletely aroused, and that the sleepwalker is in a partially awake/partially asleep state. This would fit with the idea of the brain's sleep circuits not being fully developed.

Diathesis-stress
We noted above that genetic factors cannot account on their own for sleepwalking. **Diathesis-stress** is a popular model in psychology, and proposes that a genetic vulnerability interacts with environmental factors to produce, for instance, sleepwalking. Critical factors might include sleep deprivation and tiredness, and stress.

Essential notes

The psychodynamic approach can be applied to sleepwalking, but has little or no support.

Examiners' notes

Make sure you check the number of AO1 marks available for every question and whether you need to cover more than one disorder. Adjust the number of explanations and detail to the marks available in order to gain maximum marks.

Examiners' notes

Diathesis-stress is an excellent model for combining genetic and non-genetic factors. It can often provide an effective integrating conclusion at the end of an answer.

Again there is no direct evidence for this explanation, partly because sleepwalking is relatively understudied. However, it combines findings from twin studies with the observation that sleepwalking in adults can be related to stress and so stress is likely to be at least involved in adult sleepwalking.

REM sleep behaviour disorder (RBD)

RBD is a rare form of sleepwalking usually occurring after the age of 50. It affects more men than women (Breedlove *et al.* 2007). In RBD, people do seem to act out their dreams, which is normally impossible. During REM, a centre deep in the brain, called the magnocellular nucleus, actively inhibits the muscles of the body and prevents movement. In RBD, there is evidence that the magnocellular nucleus is damaged (Culebras and Moore 1989), allowing movement during dreams and allowing the individual to act out dreams.

Legal implications

An interesting aspect of research into sleepwalking is when people accused of criminal acts claim that they were sleepwalking at the time. It is clear that genuine sleepwalkers and people with RBD are unaware of their actions and so cannot be held legally responsible. While there have been cases of acquittals based on this argument, there is also controversy as sleepwalking is relatively easy to fake. Usually the sleepwalking defence is only accepted if there is a clear clinical history of previous sleepwalking episodes.

Sleep disorders: issues, debates and approaches (IDA)

Reductionism

Biological (e.g. genetic, brain function) explanations of narcolepsy and sleepwalking are reductionist as they focus on the lowest level of explanation, ignoring higher-level psychological factors. Remember, however, that the evidence for biological explanations of narcolepsy is very powerful, while for sleepwalking it is less impressive.

Explanations for secondary insomnia usually involve precipitating factors such as medical and psychological conditions. These are not reductionist. Besides the biological approach, cognitive factors are also important, as the success of CBT for insomnia demonstrates.

Ethical issues

Much of the early work on narcolepsy involved non-human animals, raising ethical issues and the problem of generalizing findings to humans. Note, however, that research with humans has largely supported the animal work.

Free will vs determinism

The study of sleepwalking is an area where the free will vs determinism debate is very important. The key issue in a legal setting is whether sleepwalkers are responsible for their actions and can be held to account for them, or whether their actions were determined by biological factors outside their control. The practical consequences of this for people in legal disputes also makes this an example of socially sensitive research.

Examiners' notes

If you introduce possible social/legal implications of findings, make sure that you link them explicitly to the explanations you are evaluating, and refer to them clearly as implications. In this way you will access AO2/3 marks.

Examiners' notes

The secret to effective use of IDA points is to demonstrate your clear understanding of their meaning and relevance. It is better to cover a few well than simply to list lots of them in the hope that they might be relevant.

Answering A2 examination questions

AO1, AO2 and AO3

The A2 examination assesses three 'assessment objectives' known as AO1, AO2 and AO3:

- AO1 assesses your ability to recall and show your understanding of scientific knowledge – e.g. describing a theory or study.
- AO2 assesses your ability to analyse and evaluate scientific knowledge – e.g. evaluating a theory in terms of research support.
- AO3 is concerned with 'How Science Works' – e.g. methodological criticisms of research studies.

Be prepared

A2 questions will often occur as questions in parts and these different parts can also occur with different mark allocations. For example, question (a) on a particular topic could be worth:

- 4, 5 or 9 marks (for exams up to 2011), or
- 4 or 8 marks (for exams from 2012 onwards).

This means that not only should you be aware of all the topics on which you may be questioned, but you should also have practised examination type answers for these to fit the varying mark allocations.

For example, if you have covered the Unit 3 topic of biological rhythms and sleep, and included restoration theory as one of your theories of sleep, then you should be able to produce a 'shorter version' outline of the theory to answer a shorter 4- or 5-mark question, as well as being able to produce a 'longer version' outline of the explanation for an 8- or 9-mark question. This has two clear benefits:

- You will have the information you need to produce enough descriptive material for a higher mark allocation question.
- You won't waste valuable exam time by overproducing an answer for a smaller mark allocation.

Use your time wisely

Examinations are held under time constraints, and so you must use your time wisely. Students often waste far too much time doing things that are not required, e.g. stating *'In this essay I am going to...'* or providing irrelevant information. This means that they don't have sufficient time to do the things they should be doing, and so lose many of the marks available.

Read for understanding

When reading a question, ensure that you fully understand its requirements. Far too often, students focus in on a certain word or phrase that identifies the particular topic being examined and base their answer solely on that. After expending much time and effort, they then realize that they are not answering the question as it should be answered or discover they cannot answer the question as well as they first imagined. Therefore, make sure you have read the entire question and fully understand its requirements *before* starting to answer it.

Make a plan

When you have fully understood the question and have decided that you are able to answer it, then it's also a good idea to prepare a small plan of points to be made, possibly in bullet point form numbered in a logical order. This not only gives you a plan to follow, but also protects against forgetting some of these points mid-answer. It also helps you to engage with the material, which again is a useful strategy towards producing higher-quality answers.

Effective evaluation

Students can often become confused, especially under exam conditions, as to what to include in an answer requiring evaluation. A good way to combat this problem is to include the 'recipe' method as a regular part of your revision. Thus, when planning the evaluative content for an answer, list all the different elements that could comprise evaluation. This will vary slightly from question to question depending on the wording, but generally you should have:

- examples of research that both supports and weakens points being made
- practical applications
- IDA points (see below)
- methodological points (especially in questions specifically about research studies)
- implications
- theoretical support.

You may not actually use all of this material, but you should produce answers with good breadth of evaluation, as well as reducing the chances of having insufficient material or of using non-creditworthy material.

Issues, debates and approaches (IDA)

An important feature of the AO2 marking allocation is that examiners look for evidence of issues, debates or approaches in your answer. There are many different ways of addressing this requirement, including the following:

- *issues* – gender and cultural bias, ethical issues, real world application
- *debates* – psychology as science, reductionism, free will/ determinism, nature/nurture
- *approaches* – biological, evolutionary, psychodynamic, etc.

Opportunities for IDA are flagged up throughout this book, so it is a good idea to practise generating these for all the topics relevant to A2 relationships.

Elaboration in AO2 evaluation

AO2 assesses your ability to analyse and evaluate scientific knowledge relevant to a specific topic area. When allocating marks for AO2 questions, examiners look for appropriateness and *elaboration*. One way of elaborating effectively is to use the 'three-point rule'. This involves:

- *identifying* the critical point
- *justifying* it
- *explaining* why this is good (or bad) for the theory or explanation being evaluated.

For example, if your criticism is that a study lacks ecological validity, this point can be elaborated thus:

'This study lacks validity (*identification*), because research by X failed to replicate the findings of Y (*justification*), which therefore means that the findings of Y's research cannot be generalized beyond the specific situation of that experiment (*explanation*)'.

Using the right terminology

As well as having a good understanding of psychological concepts and topics, you also need to be able to communicate your understanding to others. A useful and simple means of achieving this is by using psychological terminology wherever relevant in exam answers. Try to develop a good working knowledge of psychological terminology throughout your studies – and practise using it – in order to become proficient in this skill. However, be careful not to use jargon for its own sake, as this can lead to the danger of writing incomprehensible answers that appear muddled.

Example questions and answers with examiner comments

On the following pages you will find sample questions followed by sample average and strong answers, and also tinted boxes containing the comments and advice of examiners. Answers refer to content within the revision section of this book and additional content, providing you with the opportunity to consolidate and extend your revision and research.

Examiners' notes

It is worth placing obvious 'tags' on your evaluation to make sure the examiner acknowledges it as such. For example, instead of just *describing* a supporting research study, you should preface any such description with a phrase such as 'This claim is supported by research by... which showed that...'.

Examiners' notes

A characteristic of high-grade answers is that they make extensive use of appropriate psychological terminology. Hence, using terms such as 'endogenous pacemaker' rather than 'body clock' or 'REM sleep' rather than 'dream sleep' demonstrates your familiarity with these concepts and your ability to construct informed responses using the correct terminology.

Example Paper 1

Question 1

*Outline and evaluate **one or more** explanations for the functions of sleep.*
[25 marks (2009 onwards)**] [24 marks** (2012 onwards)**]**

- Before you start writing, always spend a minute working out exactly what the question requires of you, as then you can shape your response to those exact requirements.
- Here, there is a requirement for both AO1 ('outline') and AO2 ('evaluate'). Although it is not stated in the question, 8 marks of this (9 prior to 2012) are for AO1 and 16 marks for AO2. As with all Unit 3 questions, that means one-third AO1 content and two-thirds AO2 content.

- The question invites you to cover 'one or more' explanations. It is entirely up to you whether you cover one or more than one. There is no hidden catch to this invitation: one explanation offers the chance to write in more depth, whereas more than one offers more breadth. Both approaches can bring full marks.
- The most obvious explanations for this would be evolutionary theories and restoration theories. Material relating to the *nature* of sleep would not be creditworthy.

Average answer

The two types of theories I am going to write about are evolutionary theories and then restoration theories. The restoration theory claims that when we are awake, we use up biological resources so we need to sleep to restore them. Oswald (1980) claimed that REM sleep is when the brain recovers from the day, and NREM sleep is when the body recovers and is restored. The importance of REM sleep is supported by the fact that babies have a great deal of REM sleep at a time when brain development is at its fastest. Oswald also claims that there is a surge of growth hormone during NREM sleep. This is essential for the body to repair its physiological systems. A second restoration theory is by Horne. He claimed that REM and deep NREM sleep were both important for the restoration of brain processes. He called this 'core sleep'. He claimed that light NREM was 'optional sleep' and of no use for bodily restoration. This took place when people were relaxed rather than asleep.

One of the studies supporting this theory was carried out by Rechstaffen *et al.* They found that rats who are prevented from sleeping eventually die. However, it could be the stress of keeping them awake that leads to their death rather than the lack of sleep. Other support comes from a condition known as fatal familial insomnia, which is an inherited condition that stops people from sleeping, and then they tend to die within two years. ☛

The most noticeable thing about the first two paragraphs in this answer (devoted to restoration theory) is that the student has failed to structure the material into the necessary one-third AO1 to two-thirds AO2. In fact, there is slightly less AO2 material than AO1 material. The first paragraph is almost entirely AO1, and is a decent summary of both Oswald and Horne's slightly different ideas about the restorative nature of sleep.

This condition is caused by damage to the thalamus, so it is just as possible that death was due to this rather than lack of sleep. Finally, Oswald claimed that NREM sleep was for bodily restoration. In a study of ultra marathons, where people used a lot of bodily resources, they did not sleep significantly more the next day. Horne's theory is supported by studies of sleep deprivation, which showed that this affected brain functions rather than bodily functions.

The second type of theory is the evolutionary theory. For example, the hibernation theory of sleep claims that animals sleep when it is too difficult to move about and feed. This happens at night, because most animals have adapted to feed during the daytime. Therefore, they are more likely to sleep at night when it is dark. Sleeping also means that they save energy, so this means that sleep is valuable for these animals. Another evolutionary theory claims that animals sleep to keep themselves safe from predators. If they are asleep, they are still and so less likely to be conspicuous to predators.

There is support for evolutionary theories. Hibernation theory is supported by the fact that animals with very high metabolism rates have to sleep more because they use up so much energy while feeding. Animals with lower metabolism rates do not have to sleep so much because they don't use as much energy. The theory that sleep keeps animals safe from predators is supported by the fact that predator species (such as cats) sleep more than prey species (such as mice). However, it is not clear why animals would have evolved a mechanism that would also make them more vulnerable while asleep, when they could simply keep still and not be seen.

This second (AO2) paragraph covers four points, but none of them in much detail, so the points don't have as much impact as they would have if they had been elaborated and this will lower the number of marks awarded. There is nothing wrong with the studies used, but they have simply not been used effectively. It would have been better to concentrate on just three critical points and to elaborate them; even so, more AO2 material is needed, as there are twice as many AO2 marks available as AO1.

This second type of theory (evolutionary) follows a similar pattern to the first, i.e. not enough AO2 material relative to the AO1 material. Again, the AO1 content is decent enough, although it lacks the detail necessary for high AO1 marks.

This AO2 paragraph covers three points – accurately, but not in much detail. Again, more elaboration *and* more AO2 content generally are needed to push the mark into the higher mark bands. For example, no research support is offered for these points; this would have added valuable elaboration and would have made the points appear less speculative and better informed.

Average answer: overall comment

The student has missed out on many of the AO2 marks available, through lack of content and lack of elaboration. It is mainly this that keeps the answer to about Grade C/D standard.

Exam practice

Strong answer

Evolutionary explanations for sleep stress that sleep is adaptive. If sleep did not have an important adaptive function, then it would have been selected out through natural selection. Webb (1974) suggests that an important function of sleep is that it conserves energy, particularly for species that are not adapted to forage at a particular time of day (the hibernation theory). Sleeping at a time when an animal cannot forage saves energy, and so conserves calories. Webb's theory suggests that if animals did not sleep, they would need to eat more food than animals that could sleep. Over the course of evolution, natural selection would therefore have favoured animals that could sleep.

Webb's theory is supported by the observation that animals sleep more at times when food is scarce, so conserving energy at times when it cannot easily be replaced is an adaptive response (Berger and Phillips 1995). Berger and Philips also note that the bodies of mammalian species drop by two degrees when they sleep, which conserves energy. Also, small animals, which have a higher metabolic rate (which burns up more energy), sleep more than larger animals with lower metabolic rates. This makes sense because sleeping conserves energy for species that burn up a lot of calories when active.

Meddis (1975) claimed that sleep was also adaptive because it kept animals safe from predation. The absence of light at night-time and the lower temperatures makes life more dangerous, so it is more adaptive for animals to remain hidden and motionless at night, as well as saving their energy. Meddis claimed that the amount of time animals spend sleeping depends on how safe they are while sleeping and also how much time they need to spend feeding. For example, herbivores such as sheep graze on low-quality grass and so must spend a great deal of their time foraging. Also, because they are out in the open, they are not particularly safe, and therefore do not sleep a great deal. Carnivores, on the other hand, feed on nutritious meat and have safe sleeping habits, so they can sleep for far longer.

A problem with this theory is that if being safe from predators is the main function of sleep, then it would make more sense if the animal was quiet but still alert rather than unconscious through sleep. This is particularly problematic because the amount of ☞

The balance of AO1 to AO2 is passable in these two paragraphs, as there is more AO2 than AO1 but not quite the ideal 2 to 1 ratio. However, this is corrected in the next couple of paragraphs, so overall in the essay the ratio is just right.

The AO1 is clear, accurate and describes hibernation theory in the appropriate level of detail in a question that aims to cover two evolutionary theories.

The AO2 covers three points in a reasonable level of detail, but does add some research to make this more informed than speculative. Examiners are fairly realistic when it comes to material like this. If there isn't that much to write about, they don't have unrealistic expectations about how much they can expect.

Meddis's theory is covered in more detail. Again, the AO1 material is accurate and well-detailed and easily worth a mark in the top mark band.

energy saved when an animal is quiet is about the same as when it is asleep, yet it is much more vulnerable when asleep. This theory also fails to explain why animals have different types of sleep. Research by Allison and Cicchetti (1976) examined sleep patterns across 50 species and confirmed the prediction that predators have longer sleep time than prey species – carnivores sleep longer than herbivores, and animals with safe sleeping places have more sleep than animals with more dangerous sleeping places. These findings show that ecological factors are important in determining sleeping patterns. However, this research is only correlational, and so cannot tell us whether these different factors caused the differences in sleeping patterns. For example, all predators are carnivores, but not all carnivores are predators – their sleeping habits are, therefore, likely to be determined by a number of different factors. This means that evolutionary explanations are not reductionist, as they do not reduce sleep to just one factor. The theory that sleep would have evolved to keep animals safe from predators is also supported by the observation that the major organs (e.g. heart, brain) do not require 'down periods' having evolved as continuous operation mechanisms. Similarly, trees and other plant life do not require a period of sleep because darkness presents no threat to them.

The AO2 is extremely comprehensive and shows a really good critical understanding of the material. For example, the student goes way beyond merely describing the Allison and Cicchetti research, and looks at the implications of this research as well as its limitations.

There is lots of interesting material here *and* the student has elaborated it all. This is impressive and well-informed AO2 and there is lots of it.

Strong answer: overall comment

There is an excellent overall balance of AO1 and AO2 and an impressive grasp of evolutionary theories of sleep. The student avoids just speculating about the adaptive functions of sleep or making unsubstantiated claims, so this answer fully deserves a Grade A.

Question 2

Part (a)

Outline the nature of sleep. [**5 marks** (2009 onwards)] [**4 marks** (2012 onwards)]

- The most obvious way to answer this part of the question is to cover the different *types* of sleep (e.g. REM and NREM sleep) and the differences between these. Also appropriate would be the *stages* of sleep and the differences between them.
- As this question is an 'outline' injunction, it requires AO1 description only (i.e. no evaluation). Likewise, there is no need to *explain* sleep, just describe what it involves.

- The allocation of marks is relatively low, so you should avoid writing more than is needed to gain those marks. About 100 to 120 words would be sufficient.
- When describing the nature of REM sleep, be careful not to wander too far into a discussion of dreaming.

Average answer

Sleep can be divided into different stages. Stage 1 is when the person first falls asleep and the person can be woken fairly easily. Stage 2 sleep is slightly deeper and the EEG changes. Stage 3 is deeper still and the person is difficult to wake up. Stage 4 is the deepest level of sleep and EEG is very slow. It is very difficult to wake the person during this stage. The final stage is REM sleep, which is when the eyes move rapidly and the person dreams. The person has four or five of these cycles every night.

This is accurate enough, but lacks depth and precision. For example, the claim that stage 2 is 'deeper' is pretty meaningless, as is the claim that EEG 'changes'. What is here would certainly be worth around half the available marks, but with a little more precision in the description, it could have secured all the available marks.

Strong answer

Sleep can be divided into two main types, REM (rapid eye movement) sleep and Non-REM sleep. NREM sleep, also known as slow-wave sleep, has four stages. Stages 1 and 2 are the lighter stages of sleep, and stages 3 and 4 are the deeper stages of sleep. Each stage is characterized by a change in EEG patterns, and as a person moves through the stages, they become more difficult to wake. It takes about one hour to move through the four stages, and the person then enters REM sleep. The EEG pattern in REM sleep is very similar to that when the person is awake, and REM sleep is often accompanied by dreaming.

This answer shows a clear and accurate understanding of the different stages of sleep. The difference between these stages is perfectly appropriate for an answer worth just 5 marks (4 marks from 2012). Detail is added with mention of EEG patterns and difficulty of waking. This answer is worth full marks for this part of the question.

Part (b)

*Outline and evaluate **one or more** explanations for narcolepsy.* [**4 marks + 16 marks**]

This question requires some careful planning before diving in to answer it.

- First, there are only 4 marks available for AO1, and 16 (i.e. *four times* as many) for AO2. This translates into about 100 to 120 words for the AO1 content and 400 to 480 for the AO2 content. Remember that these are only guidelines, because length of answer does not necessarily indicate quality.
- The question asks specifically for *explanations* of narcolepsy, i.e. not descriptions of it, or explanations of any other type of sleep disorder.
- The question asks for *one or more* explanations. If you go for the 'or more' option, this helps when constructing your AO2 response as it gives you more to write about. However, this makes it more problematic when constructing your AO1 response because you only have 100 to 120 words available.

- This is a challenging question, especially in terms of providing high-quality AO2. However, there are lots of opportunities for AO2, e.g. research evidence, evidence using animals, autopsy evidence, treatment implications and so on. Most students become (understandably) reliant on their textbooks when revising for an exam, but you can always supplement the information there with your own reading to ensure you are well prepared for even the most challenging of questions such as this.
- IDA points for this question could centre round issues to do with research using non-human animals and real-life applications of research in finding effective treatments for narcolepsy.

Average answer

Narcolepsy is a term used to describe a condition where the individual has periods of excessive sleepiness during the day. The symptoms of narcolepsy are that cataplexy may occur where the muscles go into paralysis. This often happens following a strong emotion, such as when the person has been laughing or even when they are having sex. People who suffer from narcolepsy also experience hypnagogic hallucinations which they find difficult to distinguish from reality.

The REM explanation for narcolepsy is that neurons that usually become active when the person is in REM sleep suddenly become active when the person is awake. When a person is in REM sleep, they enter a state of muscle paralysis, so if this happens while the person is awake, they would collapse. This explanation is supported by Vogel (1960), who found that narcoleptics went straight into a state of REM sleep after they went to sleep. There is also evidence from studies of dogs. Siegel (1999) found that nerve cells in the brains of narcoleptic dogs that were active only during REM sleep in normal animals were active during wakefulness in these dogs. This suggests that narcolepsy is caused by a problem with that part of the nervous system that normally controls REM sleep. ☞

This first paragraph is a description of narcolepsy and its symptoms – but this is *not* required by the question, and so it is wasted time and receives no marks. It is a common mistake that students make, because they *want* to describe narcolepsy, but there is no part of the question that asks you to do this.

The REM explanation is appropriate as an explanation of narcolepsy, as problems with neurons in the medulla have been implicated with the characteristics of narcolepsy. The material is reasonably accurate and there is the appropriate balance of AO1 and AO2, so this paragraph does bring the answer back on track. Note that the last sentence may seem like a very obvious thing to say (and so not worth saying), but it does draw a conclusion and is creditworthy.

Another explanation is that narcolepsy is to do with an individual having unacceptable sexual impulses. In a narcoleptic episode, these fantasies are blocked on a neuromuscular level and so the person collapses. Morgenstern (1965) did provide some evidence for this explanation. He studied a man with narcolepsy and found that he also had a hysterical disorder that was a product of his unacceptable impulses. He also experienced cataplexy at orgasm, which further supports the claim that narcolepsy and unacceptable sexual impulses are somehow linked.

A final explanation is that people with narcolepsy have very low levels of hypocretin. Studies of narcoleptic dogs have shown that these dogs have a particular gene that leads them to have very low levels of hypocretin, and this could be what is causing their narcolepsy. However, it seems unlikely that the low levels of hypocretin found in humans are caused by genetic factors. One of the reasons for this is that if one twin has narcolepsy, the chances of the other twin having narcolepsy are no greater than the risk for the general population. Because narcoleptics have low levels of hypocretin, it should be possible to treat the disorder by administering a drug that restores hypocretin levels.

The student has struggled with this explanation. It is now a largely discredited explanation, but it is still an explanation, so would be creditworthy. It is a difficult explanation to describe and even more difficult to evaluate, so, not surprisingly, this paragraph is not as effective as the previous one. As a general rule, if you intend to include something in an answer, you need to have sufficient descriptive and evaluative material to form an effective response to the question. The material in this paragraph is only partly formed.

This is a reasonably competent précis of the role of hypocretin. It is not as sophisticated as the 'Strong answer' on pp. 49–50, but forms a much smaller proportion of the total answer. It is accurate enough, although lacks precision at times (e.g. how hypocretin levels might be restored and how this might 'treat' narcolepsy). By trying to include so many explanations, the answer has become rather superficial.

Average answer: overall comment

This was always going to be a challenging question, but the student has had a good go at it, including three distinct explanations. However, none of these go into much detail, and the description of the nature of narcolepsy at the beginning of the question was unnecessary. This would be a Grade D standard essay.

Strong answer

Narcolepsy is thought to result from abnormal hypocretin functioning. Hypocretin levels have been found to be very low in patients with narcolepsy. Hypocretin regulates activity in the hypothalamus, which is a part of the brain associated with sleep. Hypocretins play an important role in maintaining wakefulness. Having a deficiency of hypocretin can trigger the sleep attacks found in narcolepsy individuals. Mignot *et al.* (1999) found that most patients with narcolepsy do not have abnormal hypocretin gene mutations, which explains why narcolepsy in humans is not genetic to the same extent it is in dogs. This suggests that the cells that normally secrete hypocretin must have been destroyed, and this leads to abnormal sleep attacks. The reason why these cells die is thought to be due to an abnormality in the immune system.

Evidence for the role of hypocretin in canine narcolepsy was discovered by Mignot *et al.* (1999). They found that these dogs had a mutation in a hypocretin receptor gene, which caused canine narcolepsy. Mignot *et al.* (2007) attempted to breed a colony of narcoleptic zebra fish by obtaining mutant fish that lacked hypocretin receptors. However, they did not respond in the same way as narcoleptic humans, and therefore did not provide insights into the role played by hypocretin in human narcolepsy. This shows the limitation of using animals to try to understand human behaviour. The hypocretin cells of the zebra fish are not organized in the same way as they are in mammals so their validity in understanding the causes of human narcolepsy is limited. However, there is evidence for the importance of hypocretin in human narcolepsy from Thannickal *et al.* (2000). They found that the brains of individuals with narcolepsy contain less than 10% of the usual complement of hypocretin neurons, and their cerebrospinal fluid had no measurable level of hypocretin. This reinforces the claim that low levels of hypocretin are associated with the development of narcolepsy.

The important role played by hypocretins has implications for the treatment of narcolepsy. As most cases of human narcolepsy show that the patients are hypocretin deficient, hypocretin replacement therapy appears to be a suitable option for treatment. There is some evidence for the effectiveness of this treatment in animals. Intravenous administration of hypocretin ☛

This student has chosen to concentrate on the role played by hypocretin, although there is also some reference to the role of genetics. This is adventurous but perfectly acceptable. It allows them to offer a good level of detail in this first AO1 paragraph. This is accurate and appropriately detailed and earns good marks for AO1. The danger may be that they do not have enough to write about for AO2 (which should be four times the length of this AO1 section), but read on …

This is a very well-informed and effective AO2 paragraph. Most of the direct experimental evidence for the role of hypocretin does come from animal studies, but the student has gone beyond this and discussed the limitations of animal studies for understanding human narcolepsy. This also satisfies the IDA requirements of the question.

The final point is an excellent example of the three-point rule. The student has *identified* the critical point ('However, there is evidence for the importance of hypocretin…'), *justified* it ('They found that the brains of individuals with narcolepsy…') and then *elaborated* it ('This reinforces the claim that…'). This makes the evaluation far more effective and ensures a mark in the higher mark bands.

in dogs has been shown to lead to increased activity (Siegel *et al.* 2001), and injections of hypocretins in rats increased the time the animals spent awake (Sakurai 2007). Nishino and Okuro (2010) claim, however, that administration of hypocretin is not that effective in the treatment of narcolepsy because it does not cross the blood brain barrier. They suggest that treatment options for narcolepsy are also currently limited (e.g. the use of stimulants) because they treat the symptoms not the cause of the narcolepsy. Modafinil, when used in the treatment of narcolepsy, is believed to activate hypocretin-containing neurons, thus helping patients stay awake during the day. Evidence for the effectiveness of modafinil in the treatment of narcolepsy comes from a study by Broughton *et al.* (1997). An additional advantage of modafinil is that it has less potential for abuse than stimulant drugs, which are the other present drug treatment for narcolepsy.

Low levels of hypocretin are probably not due to inherited factors because human narcolepsy does not run in families, and there is not a high concordance rate in twins where one has the disorder (Mignot 1998). The lack of a genetic link in narcolepsy suggests that there is nothing wrong genetically, and that the low level of hypocretin is probably due to an autoimmune disorder (Thannickal *et al.* 2000).

This is another effective AO2 paragraph based around the implications of hypocretin deficiency for the treatment of narcolepsy. This is again appropriate and suitably elaborated (i.e. all the critical points are developed), and every critical point is used effectively in the construction of the overall critical commentary. It is worth emphasizing that evaluation can also be positive, as it identifies suitable treatments that might be derived from this research. There is also some IDA credit in this paragraph, in that it is looking at real-life applications of our understanding of the causes of narcolepsy, i.e. developing effective treatments for the disorder.

Perhaps the genetic link in hypocretin could have been elaborated a little more, but the overall amount and quality of the AO2 material presented here is of a very high standard.

Strong answer: overall comment

This is a very ambitious essay and shows an excellent level of understanding – both descriptive *and* evaluative – that is easily worth a mark in the top mark band for both AO1 and AO2. The balance between the two is appropriate and the student has constructed an extremely well-informed response to the question. This is a clear Grade A.

Question 3

Part (a)

Outline lifespan changes in sleep. [**5 marks** (2009 onwards)] [**4 marks** (2012 onwards)]

- This short question requires a brief précis (about 100–120 words) of how sleep patterns change over the lifespan. This might include changes in overall length of sleep (that decreases with age) or changes in the proportion of different types of sleep.

- Note that the question requires an outline of lifespan changes only – not the *nature* of sleep or the *functions* of sleep. You could, however, include research evidence to elaborate the claims being made.

Average answer

There are lifespan changes in how much people sleep as they get older. Young babies spend most of their day sleeping rather than awake. When they get a bit older, they spend less time sleeping and more time awake. Research has suggested that teenagers actually need more hours of sleep than adults, who generally need eight hours a night. As people get older, they sleep less, until when they become very old, when they have very poor-quality sleep but have frequent cat-naps during the day. There are also differences in the amount of REM sleep that people have at different ages, with younger people having more REM sleep than older people.

This is an almost 'commonsensical' answer that lacks detail and evidence. However, it is sufficiently accurate to be worth about half the marks available. The student could have added a bit of the detail (e.g. of sleep proportions) to push this mark upwards. For example, as this is a question on 'lifespan changes', we might expect something a little more detailed than merely asserting that 'younger people have more REM sleep than older people'.

Strong answer

In the newborn baby, REM sleep accounts for over half the total sleep time. As children age, this reduction in the proportion of REM to total sleep time continues with young adults having 20% of total sleep time in REM and older adults (aged 70+) having only 10% of their sleep in REM. There is also a reduction in total time sleeping as people age, mostly in the amount of time people spend in stages 3 and 4. People over 60 have half as much stage 3 and 4 sleep compared to someone of 20. Breedlove *et al.* (2007) found that people over the age of 90 lose these stages of sleep completely.

This student has focused very much on the 'statistics' of lifespan changes in sleep, which is absolutely fine. We are given statistics about lifespan changes in REM sleep and Stage 3 and 4 sleep. This is detailed and accurate, and would be worth the maximum marks available for this part of the question.

Part (b)

Discuss the role of endogenous pacemakers in the control of biological rhythms. [**4 marks + 16 marks**]

- This is a fairly common mark division in Unit 3 part questions, i.e. 4 marks for AO1 and 16 for AO2. This seems a little strange at first, because there is a natural tendency to describe something in as much detail as it is evaluated. However, that would not be appropriate here, so don't waste time with too much descriptive material.
- The most obvious inclusion for endogenous pacemakers would be the suprachiasmatic nucleus (SCN) and the associated pathways. There would also be a case for some discussion of exogenous zeitgebers, but only insofar as they interact with endogenous pacemakers.
- Note that the question asks for 'biological rhythms' in the plural, which indicates that more than one should be covered. The main one would be the circadian rhythm with perhaps a brief mention of how endogenous pacemakers do (or do not) control infradian rhythms.

- The plural in 'endogenous pacemakers' would be covered by discussing the SCN and its associated neural pathways, but might also include the role of the pineal gland. The important role of the pineal gland in secreting melatonin as part of the sleep/waking cycle would help to satisfy this 'plurality' requirement in the question.
- This question offers scope to bring in IDA issues such as a reliance on research using non-human animals and the issues associated with that (ethical issues, generalizability to humans).
- In exams from 2012 onwards, questions about endogenous pacemakers and exogenous zeitgebers will ask specifically about their role in the control of *circadian* rhythms, rather than biological rhythms generally. In answering such questions, you would need to focus your answer on circadian rhythms, but could bring in other biological rhythms as commentary – e.g. by pointing out that the interaction between endogenous pacemakers and exogenous zeitgebers is less important in infradian rhythms.

Average answer

Endogenous pacemakers are the body's internal clocks. The main pacemaker is the supercharismatic nucleus. This coordinates the body's circadian rhythms such as the sleep/waking cycle and body temperature. The supercharismatic nucleus is stimulated by light coming in from the eyes. This leads to the production of a hormone called melatonin, which is important in the sleep/waking cycle. When melatonin levels fall, the individual feels ready to sleep. When melatonin levels rise again in the morning, the person starts to wake up again.

There are two types of study that have explored endogenous pacemakers. The first of these uses animals. For example, there was a study that used hamsters that had shorter biological rhythms than usual. The researchers then took their supercharismatic nuclei and transplanted them into normal hamsters. They found that these hamsters then had the same biological rhythms as the other hamsters. Another study that used chipmunks (DeCoursey) removed the supercharismatic nuclei of the chipmunks. When they put them back ☛

This answer is not as accurate as the 'Strong answer' on pp. 54–5. There is a misspelling of suprachiasmatic nucleus (which is quite common, but not that important). The abbreviation SCN could have been used after the first mention rather than using up time misspelling this long word! The relationship between light and SCN is evident, as is the role of melatonin in the sleep/waking cycle. However, this has been put the wrong way around (i.e. high levels of melatonin produces sleep, low levels induce waking). There is some credit for knowing that the SCN stimulates the production of melatonin, but a more accurate description would have gained more marks.

in their natural environment, they were quickly killed because they were awake feeding when they should have been asleep in their burrows. There are problems with using animals because their physiology is different to that of humans and so we don't know whether humans are as reliant on their SCN for sleeping. There are other reasons why people sleep at night that may have nothing to do with the SCN. For example, people go to bed when it gets to a certain time. Also there are ethical issues with using animals. It is ethically wrong to use animals in this way. Animals have rights not to be used in experiments and they cannot give their informed consent in the way that human beings can.

Another type of study involved American submariners (Kelly *et al.* 1999). On nuclear submarines they stay submerged for many months and have 6-hour shifts with 12 hours off duty. This meant that they had to create an artificial day of 18 hours. They tried to make an artificial day for these men, setting meal times, and using artificial lights to simulate night and day. However, it didn't work and the men's circadian rhythms stayed at about 24 hours. This showed that the supercharismatic nucleus was more important in sleep/waking than artificial factors. Another relevant study is the cave study where a French caver called Michel Siffre lived in a cave for 6 months. His circadian rhythms stayed fairly close to 24 hours (25 hours) even though there was no natural light to reset them each day. There is a problem with this because not everybody might react in the same way as Siffre, so we can't draw conclusions from this study and apply them to everybody.

This is a reasonable answer covering three relevant studies. What lets it down is the relative lack of elaboration and the failure to include relevant AO2 material. Remember that with a 4/16 mark division, four-fifths of the total answer should be AO2 content, so the critical nature of these points needs to be stressed at all times.

This has not really happened in the first 'hamster study', though it have been relatively easy to point out explicitly *what* these studies provided evidence for. The student does mention the ethical issues concerning use of non-human animals, but the material is a little too general and is not specifically located in the context of these particular animal studies.

The submarine study is relevant but, again, more could have been made of it. The same is true of the Siffre study; the material included is mostly descriptive. A fairly superficial evaluative point is made at the end about lack of reliability; this could have been elaborated by referring to the comparable evidence from Aschoff and Wever's studies.

Average answer: overall comment

Overall, this is a reasonable answer, but it is fairly short and the AO2 material is not always used in a truly evaluative way. This would be equivalent to a Grade C answer to this question.

Strong answer

The main endogenous pacemaker is the suprachiasmatic nucleus (SCN). The SCN is stimulated by light coming from the retina, which acts as an exogenous zeitgeber. The SCN regulates the activity of the pineal gland, which produces melatonin. When light levels decrease, the SCN responds by increasing the secretion of melatonin. When light levels rise again, this stimulates the SCN to decrease melatonin secretion, and the person wakes. If the SCN is damaged, then circadian rhythms are disrupted. The interaction between endogenous pacemakers and exogenous zeitgebers is less important for infradian rhythms such as the human menstrual cycle.

Much of the research on endogenous pacemakers has been carried out on non-human animals. The important role played by the SCN has been demonstrated in animal studies. Morgan (1995) selectively bred hamsters that had 'mutant' circadian rhythms of 20 hours rather than the normal rhythm of 24 hours. They then transplanted the SCNs of these hamsters into 'normal' hamsters, who then showed the 'mutant' 20-hour rhythms. DeCoursey et al. (2000) removed the SCN of chipmunks who were then returned to the wild. A group of control chipmunks with intact SCNs were also released into the wild. After 80 days, may more of the chipmunks without SCNs had been killed by predators, because without an SCN they stayed awake foraging and were easier to locate by nocturnal predators.

There are a number of problems with using animal studies in this area. The first problem is the harm to the animals concerned. However, there is a costs-benefits consideration to research with non-human animals. The costs to the animals (e.g. DeCoursey's chipmunks were made more vulnerable to predators as a result of being used in the study) can be balanced by the possible benefits of understanding the important role played by the SCN. There is also the issue of generalization to humans. It is problematic to generalize animal findings direct to human beings because of differences in the biological systems of different species. For example, in reptiles and birds, light acts directly on the pineal gland, whereas in humans, this process is mediated by the SCN. This questions the value of findings from animal studies.

For ethical reasons it is difficult to carry out the same experiments on human beings (i.e. removing the SCN in order to study the effect on circadian rhythms) as ☞

This is a very competent first paragraph: focused, detailed and accurate. The student has correctly identified the SCN as the main endogenous pacemaker and has also made an appropriate reference to the pineal gland. They have correctly described the SCN influence on the secretion of melatonin and identified the interaction between endogenous pacemakers and exogenous zeitgebers. This is clearly worth full marks for the AO1 component of this question.

It is difficult to generate a lot of material to support this answer, as questions may more typically include both endogenous pacemakers and exogenous zeitgebers, thus giving a greater scope of material. However, this student uses material very sensibly, beginning with a discussion of studies of non-human animals, showing how they support the role of the SCN as an endogenous pacemaker.

This strong answer is followed by a good critical discussion of the use of non-human animals, which is placed effectively within the context of endogenous pacemaker research. There is always a danger of making unsubstantiated assertions about the value of animal research, but this student has avoided that in favour of informed commentary. This also counts as IDA (issues, debates and approaches) content.

this would cause physical harm to human participants. However, other studies have supported the important role played by the SCN. Michel Siffre spent 179 days in a cave in Texas, deprived of any natural light to reset his SCN each day. Siffre's sleep/waking cycle became erratic but eventually settled down to between 25 and 37 hours. They also monitored physiological measures such as heart rate and body temperature, which were also found to fluctuate on the longer cycle. This tells us that the SCN naturally runs a little slower than 24 hours, and must be corrected each day by exposure to natural daylight.

Finally, the Siffre study is also used to good effect – as evidence to support the role of the SCN – and is appropriately built into a critical commentary.

Strong answer: overall comment

Accurate, detailed and informed, this is an excellent answer. This student shows that the best answers are not always the longest answers and this is clearly worth a Grade A.

Example Paper 2

Question 1

Discuss the disruption of biological rhythms. [**25 marks** (2009 onwards)] [**24 marks** (2012 onwards)]

- As with all questions on Unit 3, there is a set division of marks between AO1 (8 marks from 2012; 9 marks prior to 2012) and AO2 (16 marks). What counts as AO1 and what counts as AO2 can be quite difficult to determine, and largely depends on what *you* determine to be AO1 and AO2.
- One way of organizing material is as follows. For AO1, you could *describe* the effects of disruption (e.g. jet lag, shift work) and the mechanisms of this disruption (e.g. disruption of the relationship between endogenous pacemakers and external zeitgebers). This would constitute the AO1 component of the answer.

- You could then use research evidence as AO2 evaluation of these effects and mechanisms. It would also be acceptable to include some reference to treatments (e.g. attempts to overcome the problems of shift work and/or jet lag), but only if you use this *explicitly* as commentary on disruption of biological rhythms, rather than a description of treatment options alone.
- Real-life examples (e.g. Three Mile Island) always make a dramatic impact on students, but are not actual psychological studies and so do not have the same scientific value as properly controlled studies.

Average answer

The most famous study in which biological rhythms were disrupted was carried out by Michel Siffre. Siffre spent six months in a cave in Texas. He was wired up so that researchers could tell what his body was doing (i.e. his physiological functions). The artificial lighting was also controlled by the researchers, but Siffre had no natural daylight. To begin with, his sleeping patterns were erratic, but gradually he settled down to a regular sleep/wake pattern of between 25 and 30 hours. When he eventually came out of the cave, he had been down there for 179 days, but he had only had 151 'days' because his days were longer.

This study is important because it shows that when biological rhythms are left to be 'free running' (i.e. without the influence of natural daylight to reset them every day), they result in a longer circadian rhythm than the 24 hours we are used to. However, this is the study of just one man, and it is a very unusual study so we must be cautious about generalizing out too much to other people. There are other similar studies where people have cut themselves off from natural daylight for an extended period (e.g. Aschoff and Wever), and these also tend to show an extended circadian rhythm. This supports the claim that in order to maintain a 24-hour cycle, we need zeitgebers to reset the biological clock each day. ☞

This is a fairly common opening for essays on this topic. The story of Michel Siffre is undoubtedly fascinating, and possibly tells us a great deal about what happens when the body's endogenous pacemaker is dissociated from the external zeitgeber of natural daylight. The first paragraph would count as AO1 as it describes the study.

The second paragraph would count as AO2 as it comments on the importance of the study as well as its limitations. However, the student would have done better to summarize the main findings and/or conclusions of this study in a few sentences rather than in two long paragraphs, especially as there are much better controlled studies available (such as Aschoff and Wever (1981)), although admittedly not as extreme. The lesson here, is to be careful how much time you devote to an example such as this, as it is easy to get carried away and write far too much.

Biological rhythms can also be disrupted when we travel long distances across time zones. For example, if we fly from New York to London, when we land in London our body clock still thinks it is New York time. If we reach London at 9 a.m., the light coming through our eyes tells us that it is daytime, but our body clock (the SCN) tells us it is still the middle of the night (4 a.m. New York time) and that we should still be asleep. This means we feel tired and disoriented, because our bodily rhythms have been disrupted. There is some evidence for this from a study of baseball teams in the US that had to fly long distances to play their matches. The researchers found that they did less well when they had to fly West to East than when they had to fly East to West. They concluded that this showed that the effects of jet lag were worse when the body clock was behind external cue, and the body had to catch up. Another study looked at cabin crew who had been travelling across time zones for many years, and found that many suffered ill effects such as memory deficits and an increase in stress hormones, thus supporting the claim that disruption of biological rhythms by jet lag can have negative effects.

A final way in which biological rhythms can be disrupted is shift work, when people have to work at night when they should be asleep. This is particularly difficult because artificial light is not strong enough to reset the body clock sufficiently and so people on night shifts have trouble concentrating and staying awake, and can also suffer increases in illness. When they try to sleep during the day, they also find this difficult because there is a lot more noise and natural light filtering through the curtains. Czeisler tried to sort this out for NASA astronauts by exposing them to extreme bright artificial lights which appeared to reset their body clocks and allowed them to have a normal sleep and waking cycle even in the absence of natural day light. He has now started to apply this technology in industry so that people can adapt more easily to night shift work.

There is probably too much information about the New York to London example – a more concise summary of this would have been more effective. The baseball team example is better as it is an actual study, although we are not really told *why* travelling West to East would be more disruptive, particularly in terms of the player's circadian rhythms. The cabin crew example is also appropriate and used in a suitably AO2 way, i.e. through the use of AO2 'tags' such as 'thus supporting the claim that...'.

This is a fairly succinct coverage of the disruption of biological rhythms due to shift work, although perhaps they have focused more on the disruptive effects of shift work itself, rather than the disruption of biological rhythms that shift work produces. The evaluation is achieved through a real-world application (the work of Czeisler), which would count as IDA, although this is not particularly well detailed.

Average answer: overall comment

This is competent if not always well detailed. By spending much too long on the details of the Michel Siffre case, the student has made it difficult to go into much detail on the much more relevant psychological studies. There is nothing wrong with the selection of material, nor its accuracy. Where the student slips up is by not giving enough detail in the studies, nor enough elaboration in the evaluation. This keeps this answer down to about Grade C level.

Strong answer

Long distance jet travel can disrupt our circadian rhythms because our internal body clock is no longer synchronized with external zeitgebers such as light and dark. The effects of jet lag include feelings of tiredness and lack of concentration. These effects tend to be worse when travelling from West to East (phase advance) than East to West (phase delay). This is because when travelling from West to East the biological clock is behind local time and so has to catch up. As a result, our circadian rhythms are dramatically disrupted and the symptoms tend to be worse than when the biological clock is ahead of local time. The SCN gradually adjusts to the changed external zeitgebers, but this takes a few days.

A study that supports the claim that West–East travel is more disruptive in terms of circadian rhythms than East–West travel is Recht et al. (1995). They analysed the performance of American basball teams over three seasons and found that teams won 37% of away games when they had travelled West to East and 44% after travelling East to West. Recht et al. claimed that jet lag had affected the players' performance and that these effects were worse after phase advance than after phase delay. The problem with this study is that there are many uncontrolled variables that could influence the results, such as the ability of the other team, injuries, etc. This makes it difficult to draw definite conclusions about the effects of disrupted bodily rhythms.

Other studies have investigated the disruption of bodily rhythms in people who are regularly exposed to jet travel. Cho et al. (2000) studied aircrew and found that many had raised levels of stress hormones and performed relatively poorly on tests of memory compared to control participants. Research studies such as these confirm that jet travel can and does lead to problems with cognitive processes and stress-related illness. However, because these studies are correlational only, they do not demonstrate a cause and effect between jet travel and the symptoms associated with jet lag. Knowledge of what causes jet lag has led to an interest in treatments to ease its symptoms. For example, it is claimed that exposure to bright light can shift circadian rhythms during long distance jet travel. Boulos et al. (2002) used a head-mounted light visor on an East-West flight across six time zones. However, there was no improvement in sleep or other jet lag symptoms. ☞

This is an effective opening paragraph that would count as AO1 because it covers the *effects* of disruption (e.g. feelings of tiredness and lack of concentration) and the mechanisms (e.g. the body clock is no longer synchronized with external zeitgebers). There is sufficient detail to represent how and why jet lag is disruptive to biological rhythms.

There is a lot of appropriate AO2 material in these two paragraphs. The student has clearly demonstrated how to use research evidence to its best effect, and at the same time has included some useful AO3 references concerning the limitation that correlational data do not demonstrate a causal relationship.

The application at the end of this paragraph (use of the head-mounted visor) would count as IDA content. It is competently elaborated through the addition of supporting evidence – or, in this case, evidence that suggests the application does not work!

Shift work also disrupts circadian rhythms, because when working at night, a person must be active at a time when their biological clock is telling them to sleep. Under normal circumstances, our circadian rhythms mean that we sleep when it is dark and wake up when it is light again. However, when we work on a night shift, we are going against our circadian rhythms, trying to maintain alertness when our body is attempting to sleep. Additionally, workers on night shift must try to sleep during the daytime, when external zeitgebers such as light and distractions such as noise make sleep difficult. This means that night-shift workers also suffer from mild sleep deprivation, which makes it difficult to draw definite conclusions about the effects of disrupting biological rhythms through shift work.

The negative effects of shift work was demonstrated in a study by Gold et al. (1992), who found that nurses on nightshift had significantly more road accidents than those working during daytime. There is also evidence that the disruption of bodily rhythms through shift work is associated with an increase in the chances of developing breast cancer or heart disease (Davis et al. 2001). This is because exposure to light at night-time suppresses the normal nocturnal production of melatonin by the pineal gland. Melatonin is believed to be important in preventing tumor growth. Davis et al. found that women who frequently do not sleep when melatonin levels are usually at their highest have a 14% increase in breast cancer risk.

Knowledge of the relationship between biological rhythms and external zeitgebers, particularly light, has led to applications to cope with the negative effects. For example, Czeisler (1982) changed shift patterns at a chemical plant to make them rotate less frequently and to rotate forwards rather than backwards. He argued that one week was not long enough for resynchronization of the biological clock with the pattern of light and darkness. After nine months on the new shift pattern, there was less absenteeism and workers reported feeling less stressed, saying they had less of a problem with sleeping and fewer health problems.

This paragraph on disruption of biological rhythms as a consequence of shift work is mostly AO1 description. Rather than simply describing the problems of shift work, this student explains how and why shift work disrupts biological rhythms, and then how this disruption results in negative effects such as sleep difficulties. There is also an appropriate AO3 point at the end of the paragraph, describing how the findings of shift-work studies may be confounded by the problems of sleep deprivation.

The final two paragraphs are an excellent example of effective AO2 commentary. We are informed about the negative effects of the disruption of bodily rhythms, but then this is supported by research evidence to increase the impact of the point. For example, there is a claim that disruption is harmful because it increases the risks of breast cancer. This is not only explained in terms of the relationship between melatonin and tumour inhibition, but research evidence is also offered to support the claim.

The last paragraph presents the IDA component of the answer (remember that this is marked as AO2, rather than having a discrete mark of its own). This is elaborated through appropriate research evidence.

Strong answer: overall comment

This is an extremely well-crafted answer. It uses research evidence in appropriate ways to add detail to descriptive content (AO1) and to evaluate this material through research evidence (AO2). This is a high-quality answer that is clearly of a Grade A standard.

Question 2

Part (a)

Outline and evaluate the evolutionary explanation for the functions of sleep.
[5 marks + 8 marks (2009 onwards)] **[4 marks + 8 marks** (2012 onwards)]

- In a sense there is no such thing as the evolutionary theory of sleep so any explanation that stresses the adaptive nature of sleep would be creditworthy. For example, Webb believes that sleep is adaptive because it helps animals to conserve energy during times when foraging would be difficult. Meddis believes that the inactivity associated with sleep keeps animals safe from predators.
- Note that material on the restoration functions of sleep or the nature of sleep would *not* be creditworthy.
- When there is an indication of two separate marks available in an answer (as here), the *first* of these marks is an indication of the AO1 marks and the *second* of the marks is an indication of the AO2 marks in the question. Therefore, this question part indicates 4 marks for AO1 (5 marks prior to 2012) and 8 marks for AO2.

- Some students ignore the two instructions in a question like this ('outline and evaluate') and simply present a general essay on the functions of sleep, leaving the examiner to divide the essay on their part, allocating marks where they are appropriate. It is far more effective (and a better way of gathering marks) to separate out the two parts of the answer or even to present separate AO1 and AO2 paragraphs.
- Students often ignore the mark divisions of questions like this and assume that equal amounts of AO1 and AO2 are appropriate. Because of the unequal mark distribution, you should ensure that you present about twice as much AO2 material as AO1 material. Most students will write about 300–360 words for this question, so that means 100–120 words of AO1 and 200–240 words of AO2.
- At the other extreme, some students are so anxious to focus on AO2 that they provide only very brief accounts of relevant explanations. It's right to concentrate on the AO2 material, but do take care to provide sufficient detailed AO1 material to gain *all* the marks available.

Average answer

The main claim of the evolutionary theory of sleep is that sleep has an adaptive value, and animals are more likely to survive if they can sleep. This makes sense, because natural selection would have selected out animals that did not sleep, because they would have been less likely to survive. Webb (1992) claimed that the main adaptive function of sleep was so that the animal could conserve energy. Sleep was a form of enforced inactivity at a time when animals could not forage because they were not adapted to be active in the hours of darkness. Another evolutionary explanation is that animals sleep to keep themselves safe from predators. An animal that is asleep does not attract a predator's attention, so is safer than if moving about. According to this view, prey species would sleep less because they need to remain vigilant for predators. Predators such as lions would therefore be able to sleep a great deal. ☞

This student has not thought that much about the differential mark allocation for AO1 and AO2. There is far too much AO1 material here at the expense of the much more 'lucrative' (in terms of allocated marks) AO2. The *quality* of this material is very good, and there is lots of it, but for the low number of AO1 marks available, the investment may not prove worthwhile.

A problem for the energy conservation explanation is that when we are asleep, there is not that much difference in the amount of energy we consume compared to just being quiet and inactive. Because we are potentially more vulnerable when in a state of unconsciousness, it does not make that much sense that sleep would have evolved just to conserve energy. The idea that sleep evolved to keep animals safe from predators can be challenged by the fact that when animals are asleep, they are actually more vulnerable to predators and cannot feed or look after their young. However, some species have evolved adaptations to deal with this problem, e.g. the Indus river dolphin, which has unilateral sleep, where one hemisphere of the brain sleeps at a time.

Just as there is too much AO1, there is too little AO2. Only two evaluative points are offered here, although they are both good and well developed. The conservation of energy explanation is perhaps dismissed rather abruptly, although this is a fair point concerning the minor difference in energy consumption between waking and sleeping states. Similarly, the point concerning an increased vulnerability while asleep is elaborated with reference to adaptations that overcome this problem. The use of research evidence would have helped to develop this AO2 section. This answer would be graded around a Grade D.

Strong answer

The evolutionary theory of sleep claims there are two major functions for sleep. Webb (1974) suggests that when animals sleep, they conserve energy, particular at a time where it is not easy to forage because most animals are not adapted to be active at night-time. Because temperatures may drop below zero at night, animals may further conserve energy by communal sleeping arrangements. A second adaptive function for sleep is that sleep keeps animals safe from predation, particularly when hidden from view and motionless in a burrow or nest. Meddis (1975) claimed that the amount of time animals spend sleeping depends on how safe they are while sleeping, so animals that sleep in the open would sleep less than animals that sleep in burrows.

The energy conservation explanation is supported by the observation that animals sleep more at times when food is scarce (e.g. many species hibernate during the winter months) so they are conserving energy at times when it cannot easily be replaced (Berger and Phillips 1995). In addition, Berger and Philips note that the temperature of mammalian species' bodies drops by two degrees while they sleep, which conserves energy. This explanation is further supported by the fact that small animals that have a higher metabolic rate sleep for longer than larger animals with lower metabolic rates. This explanation fails to explain why the animal becomes unconscious during normal sleep. However, because the brain uses a large proportion of the body's calories, conservation of energy is best served by limiting its sensory inputs.

A problem with the 'safety from predation' explanation is that animals may actually be more vulnerable when completely asleep and would be safer from predators if they were quiet yet relatively active. However, some species have adapted to the need to remain vigilant while asleep, e.g. some species, such as porpoises, sleep one hemisphere at a time. Mallard ducks are able to sleep with one eye open so to remain vigilant against predators. Allison and Cicchetti (1976) looked at sleep patterns in 50 species and confirmed the prediction that prey species sleep for less time than predator species. They also confirmed that animals with safe sleeping places (such as burrows and nests) sleep longer than animals that must sleep in the open, where they would be more vulnerable to predation.

The student has decided to split their essay neatly into AO1 material in one section of the essay and AO2 in the latter section. This is not the only way to write an essay, but it does make it easier to keep track of how much of each you have written – this is very important given that the mark allocations for AO1 and AO2 are very different. This material covers two distinct aspects of the evolutionary perspective: conservation of energy and safety from predation. It is accurate and detailed and of the right length for all the AO1 marks available.

An impressive feature of this AO2 material is that the student has made sure that it really is AO2, not only by picking appropriate material, but also adding explicit AO2 'tags' for maximum impact, i.e. by using expressions such as 'This explanation is further supported by…' and 'This explanation fails to explain…'.

There is plenty of evaluative material, and it has been used effectively throughout. Impressively, the student has elaborated some of the points so that a mini discussion develops within the answer. For example, they raise the point that animals may be more vulnerable to predation when asleep, but then qualify that by discussing some of the adaptations that overcome this vulnerability. This is clearly a Grade A answer to this part of the question.

Part (b)

Outline and evaluate the restoration explanation for the functions of sleep.
[5 marks + 8 marks (2009 onwards)] **[4 marks + 8 marks** (2012 onwards)]**

- As with part (a), there is an indication here of the different number of marks available for AO1 and AO2, i.e. 4 marks for AO1 (5 marks prior to 2012) and 8 marks for AO2.
- Appropriate AO1 material would include the relative roles of REM and NREM in restoration of bodily and brain processes, and the separate views of Oswald and Horne on the role of different types of sleep for restoration of body and brain. AO2 material could include a review of evidence (e.g. sleep deprivation studies), recovery from strenuous energy, fatal familial insomnia, insights from animal studies, etc.

- Students often include cases of extreme sleep deprivation, such as Randy Gardner and Peter Tripp. These can be useful in emphasizing the speed with which people can recover from sleep deprivation, but these are uncontrolled studies and would not have the same impact as proper psychological studies.
- It is possible to include some discussion of evolutionary explanations as an alternative perspective, but only if these are built into a critical commentary rather than just being described in their own right. For example, you might discuss some way in which the evolutionary perspective offers a better explanation for a research finding than the restoration perspective.

Average answer

Oswald believed that the purpose of sleep was to restore the body after neurotransmitters and hormones have been used up during the day. The body uses sleep to repair itself. For example, when people have been very active, they will sleep longer so that the body can restore all the things that have been used up during the day. If people don't sleep, then they don't get the chance to repair their body and eventually could die.

There is evidence against restoration study from sleep deprivation studies. One study involved a schoolboy called Randy Gardner, who managed to stay awake for 11 days. He showed no harmful effects after his sleep deprivation other than a few minor effects such as incoherent speech. This shows that people do not suffer that much from sleep deprivation, which challenges Oswald's claim that sleep is essential to restore bodily processes. Another study on a DJ called Peter Tripp showed that he stayed awake for 8 days, and although he survived and was physically okay, he suffered hallucinations. Although this study seems to challenge the restoration theory because sleep deprivation did not have the effects predicted, it is possible that both Randy Gardner and Peter Tripp cat-napped during the time they were awake. ☞

There is little depth to this answer. There is a very basic understanding of the underlying claim of restoration theory (in the first sentence), but after this there is just repetition and a few inaccuracies (e.g. what studies of strenuous exercise *really* tell us about the role of sleep). This could have been improved by adding more details about *what* is restored, and the different roles played by REM and NREM sleep. The answer could also have been elaborated with inclusion of Horne's distinction between 'core' and 'optional' sleep. This answer would probably only pick up 1 or 2 of the marks available for AO1.

Students love to recount the strange tales of Randy Gardner and Peter Tripp, possibly because they seem so extreme they must tell us *something* about the effects of sleep deprivation. However, these are not studies and so are hard to make worthwhile in an exam answer. Another common mistake (as here) is to waste a lot of time describing all the peripheral details. It would have been far better to spend the time describing the more influential experimental studies of sleep deprivation.

The restoration theory is also challenged by Horne (1988), who reviewed over 50 studies of sleep deprivation. According to Horne, none of the researchers in these studies found that sleep deprivation interfered with the ability to carry out physical exercise.

These final two sentences add a little of what is missing in this evaluation – i.e. *psychological* evidence.

Average answer: overall comment

This answer is not particularly well informed and has wasted a lot of time with material that isn't worth including. There is the right proportion of AO2 to AO1, but it just isn't of high enough quality or insight. This would be around a Grade C standard.

Strong answer

Restoration theories of sleep argue that sleep is homeostatic, restoring the equilibrium of the body's physiological systems that have been active during the day. Oswald (1980) suggests that the high level of brain activity during REM sleep meant that this type of sleep was to restore brain systems. Oswald also noted that during the deeper stages of NREM sleep, there was a surge in growth hormone release, which indicated that NREM sleep was for the restoration of the body's physiological systems. Horne (1988) proposed that REM and the deeper levels of NREM sleep make up 'core sleep', which was essential for the maintenance of brain systems rather than bodily restoration, which takes place during periods of relaxed wakefulness.

Oswald's theory is challenged by the finding that strenuous exercise should make people sleep for longer (to restore physiological processes that have been active), yet this is not what happens. Breedlove *et al.* (2007) found that although in such circumstances people do fall asleep quicker than usual, they do not sleep for longer. Oswald observed that there is a surge of growth hormone during NREM sleep, and this has an important role in protein synthesis (necessary for the restoration of bodily tissue). However, Horne points out that amino acids, which are necessary to build proteins, are only available for a few hours after a meal. By the time we sleep, the level of available amino acids is low, which means that very little tissue restoration could take place during sleep, despite the release of growth hormone.

Horne's claim that core sleep is essential for brain restoration is supported by sleep deprivation research. For example, Harrison and Horne (1999) found that participants who underwent 36 hours of sleep deprivation performed significantly worse on measures of reasoning compared to participants who were not sleep deprived. However, most sleep deprivation studies take place in sleep laboratories that do not typify the real world. People are usually sleep deprived because of other stresses such as long working hours, family crises, etc. Restoration and evolutionary explanations are not competing explanations of the functions of sleep. Although sleep may be important for the maintenance of brain function, the actual pattern of sleep is a product of evolutionary factors.

This is a succinct, accurate and well-informed précis of the main claims of the restoration perspective. Oswald and Horne are both accurately represented, and the distinction between restoration of bodily processes and restoration of brain processes is made clear. The student has not wasted time with irrelevancies and at 118 words, this is an ideal length. This paragraph would earn all the marks available for the AO1 component of this part of the question.

This is an excellent critical review of the restoration perspective on the functions of sleep. Four main critical points are made here, but they are also elaborated, thereby making up an effective critical commentary rather than a superficial review of a longer 'list' of criticisms. For example, the answer discusses sleep deprivation studies that support Horne's claim that core sleep is essential for brain restoration, but this discussion is then enhanced by a critique of the *methods* used in this type of research.

A good IDA point is made at the end concerning the integration of restoration and evolutionary perspectives.

Strong answer: overall comment

Both parts of this answer are exceptionally well balanced between the AO1 and AO2 content, and material is accurate and well detailed throughout.

This is a very skilfully constructed answer and clearly worth a Grade A.

Question 3

Part (a)

*Outline the role of **one or more** exogenous zeitgebers in the control of circadian rhythms.*
[5 marks (2009 onwards)] **[4 marks** (2012 onwards)]

- This part of the question asks for an outline of 'one or more' exogenous zeitgebers in 'circadian rhythms'. Although this implies plurality in the number of rhythms outlined, the term circadian rhythms is a general one, so you do not really need to cover more than one (e.g. sleep/waking, body temperature).

- However, description of biological rhythms without relating these to exogenous zeitgebers would not be creditworthy, nor would material relating to rhythms other than circadian rhythms. Description of how zeitgebers interact with endogenous pacemakers interaction would be directly relevant to the question.

Average answer

The term 'zeitgeber' is German for 'time-giver'. Light is the main zeitgeber because every morning, exposure to daylight resets the body clock, the suprachiasmatic nucleus, and this maintains a circadian rhythm of 24 hours. Deprivation of daylight has an influence on the circadian rhythms. When Michel Siffre lived in a cave for six months, his circadian rhythms became longer than 24 hours. Another example of a zeitgeber is temperature. Some animals hibernate when the temperature drops below a certain levels, and birds may migrate in the winter.

This is a classic example of how many students begin their answers, with unnecessary information that does not explicitly relate to the question. The fact that 'zeitgeber' means 'time-giver' in German is interesting but not relevant here. The relationship between light and the SCN is creditworthy, and the illustration of the role of light in circadian rhythms through the Siffre study is just about to pick up a second mark. The hibernation example is not relevant as this is an *infradian* rhythm, not a *circadian* rhythm.

Strong answer

Light is the main zeitgeber. Exposure to natural light resets the body's circadian rhythm each morning. Light is received via the eyes by the suprachiasmatic nucleus, which causes the pineal gland to stop the release of melatonin, and the person awakes. In conditions where people are deprived of natural light, it is difficult to maintain a 24-hour circadian rhythm. People also find it difficult when they travel across time zones because they receive external light cues to wake up (or go to sleep) at times that feel strange to the body. Social interactions (such as mealtimes and the taking of medications) can also act as zeitgebers because they provide cues to the internal clock. The body may then learn to respond to these events because of patterns established in the past.

This student has clearly identified two distinct zeitgebers, light and social interactions, explaining the nature of each of these in the context of circadian rhythms. They have elaborated their answer by explaining *why* each of these is important in maintaining circadian rhythms. This is all appropriate and accurate content and is sufficiently detailed for the full quota of AO1 marks.

Part (b)

*Outline and evaluate explanations for **one** sleep disorder.* [4 marks + 16 marks]

- The mark division between AO1 and AO2 needs to be noted, as there are four times as many marks for AO2 as for AO1. This can trap unsuspecting students who may end up writing far too much AO1 material and far too little AO2 material.
- Appropriate sleep disorders include insomnia, narcolepsy and sleepwalking.
- Description of the symptoms of the chosen sleep disorder is not necessary and would not receive credit, unless explicitly linked to *explanations*.

- For the AO2 evaluation, research studies can be used to support the relevant explanations, as can discussion (and evidence) for successful treatments, provided these treatments are explicitly linked to the explanations.
- There are many opportunities to provide the necessary IDA content for this answer. These include using explanations to develop potential treatments for the chosen sleep disorder, the use of animal research to study potential causes of the disorder and so on.

Average answer

insomnia can involve problems falling asleep (initial insomnia), problems remaining asleep (middle insomnia) and waking up too early (terminal insomnia). Insomnia can also be short-term, occasional or chronic (long-lasting), where it lasts for more than one month. Primary insomnia is where the insomnia occurs on its own (e.g. the person may have developed bad sleep habits). Secondary insomnia is where the insomnia is a symptom of something else such as depression or heart disease.

Many people develop insomnia because they have poor sleeping habits. This is known as having poor sleep hygiene. Examples of poor sleep hygiene include working too late, eating a heavy meal just before bed and working in bed. It can also be caused by having bright lights in the bedroom or by watching television in bed. If an individual changes these bad habits, e.g. by relaxing prior to going to bed or taking a hot bath, then they would be more able to fall asleep and would not experience initial insomnia. Some people believe that physical exercise can help people sleep and so rid them of insomnia. There is some research evidence to back this up. Montgomery and Dennis (2002) looked at some older people with primary insomnia. They compared a group of people who followed an exercise programme to a group who did not exercise. After 16 weeks, the exercise group had a significantly improved quality of sleep, they took less time to fall asleep, and spent longer asleep, compared with the group who did no exercise. ☞

This first paragraph has too much information that simply isn't needed, describing *types* of insomnia when the question asks about *explanations* of a sleep disorder. Simply regurgitating everything you have learned about a type of sleeping disorder won't necessarily earn marks! There is some relevant material in the last two sentences (e.g. bad sleeping habits and depression/heart disease), but very little to gain AO1 marks.

The first half of this paragraph is AO1, but reads rather like a commonsense manual than a psychologically informed explanation of insomnia. This would be much better if there were a little more research evidence to make the material more authoritative. The Montgomery and Dennis study does just that and is very useful AO2.

Another explanation for insomnia is age. As people get older, they have more problems sleeping, and so they may experience this as insomnia. Research by Breedlove *et al.* supports this. This is possibly because the mechanisms involved in sleep do not work as well as people get older. However, we cannot rely on self-reports of older people about how long they sleep, because Breedlove *et al.* found that older people may take frequent cat-naps so that may make it harder for them to sleep at night.

One of the problems with studying insomnia is that people's reports of how long they sleep may be exaggerated. The only way to really study this accurately is to study them in a sleep laboratory, where the exact length of their sleep can be recorded. Also, because the person can be wired up, then other physiological measurements such as EEG can be taken. This is also a problem, because this is not a natural way to sleep, all wired up. This means that they get a worse night's sleep (because they are not used to the bed and the wires of the EEG). The sleep laboratory may be artificial in other ways as well, e.g. it may be dark and very quiet and the bed very different to the bed they usually sleep in. Also the person must sleep on their own whereas they may be used to sleeping with their husband or wife. This means that the sleep laboratory does not represent how they usually sleep so the conclusions may not be valid.

Lifespan changes are certainly a contributory factor in sleeping difficulties, although more needs to be said here about why these changes should result in insomnia. This paragraph would receive AO1 credit, but the lack of detail limits the impact (and the marks awarded) for this material.

This final paragraph is completely AO2/AO3 as it evaluates the *methodological* issues involved in the study of insomnia. The student has a good understanding of how the artificial environment of the sleep laboratory may detract from the validity of the findings of studies that are carried out in such controlled environments.

Average answer: overall comment

There is scant regard for the AO1/AO2 mark division of this part of the question, so the student loses many of the marks allocated for AO2 and spends far too long *describing* when they should be *evaluating*. Although the answer appears psychologically informed, it often reads more like a commonsense answer to the question. There simply isn't anywhere near enough AO2 evaluation and the description lacks psychological evidence to substantiate the points being made. This would probably receive a Grade D.

Strong answer

Primary insomnia is linked to a state of 'hyperarousal' (chronic physiological arousal). Heart rate and stress hormones are raised in people with primary insomnia. They also tend to show high levels of anxiety, which also increases arousal. One explanation is that a period of extreme stress leads to insomnia, which is then maintained by a high state of anxiety and arousal about not being able to sleep. Insomnia can also be a secondary effect of a number of conditions, such as depression and post-traumatic stress disorder, or the overuse of stimulants such as caffeine and alcohol. Research (e.g. Watson *et al.* 2006) has shown that some people have a genetic vulnerability, which makes it more likely that they will develop insomnia in response to these conditions.

A problem for the hyperarousal explanation is that research findings are not consistent. Some studies (e.g. Riemann *et al.* 2010) have supported the claim that people with primary insomnia are more likely to have high arousal levels compared to controls. However, other studies have failed to find any significant difference in measures of arousal between those with primary insomnia and controls. There are also gender differences in the diagnosis of both primary and secondary insomnia (Morin *et al.* 1999), which may be due to the higher levels of neuroticism and anxiety in women compared to men.

Research has suggested that one of the main causes of primary insomnia is that people may develop the belief that they will be unable to sleep. This expectation then becomes self-fulfilling because the person is tense and anxious when trying to sleep. For such people, they have learned to attribute their sleeping difficulties to insomnia. Storms and Nisbett used this idea of maladaptive attributions to develop a treatment for insomnia, the 'reverse placebo effect'. They found that insomniacs went to sleep faster than usual on nights when they took placebos they believed to be arousal pills. They attributed their arousal to the pills rather than insomnia, and so relaxed sufficiently to allow themselves to sleep.

It is also difficult to identify a causal relationship between psychological disorders and secondary insomnia. For insomnia to be a secondary consequence of depression, it has to be shown that the depression preceded the insomnia. To establish this, it is usually necessary to ☞

This is a very effective and measured response to the AO1 component of this question. The student has distinguished between explanations for primary and secondary insomnia, and provided accurate explanations for both. These are not 'in-depth' explanations but offer sufficient detail to gain all the available AO1 marks.

This is an effective examination of the link between anxiety and primary insomnia. The student has used research evidence sensibly and has also commented on the inconsistencies of research in this area. The issue of gender differences is also used effectively, as these are linked to differences in neuroticism and anxiety between males and females.

Discussion of a possible treatment for insomnia is linked to the underlying anxiety associated with maladaptive attributions. This is well developed, so gains good AO2 marks, but it also counts as IDA content as it is illustrating a real-life application based on this explanation of the *causes* of insomnia.

use self-reports from the patient, which can be unreliable as a way of establishing exactly how depression and insomnia are related for a particular individual. For example, although it might be assumed that depression has caused insomnia, some research has shown that insomnia may lead to depression (e.g. Lichstein *et al.* 2006). In addition, therapeutic interventions for insomnia have been shown to simultaneously reduce the symptoms of depression, suggesting that insomnia, rather than depression, was the primary problem (Stepanski and Rybarczyk 2006). This means that we cannot assume that a person has a secondary insomnia based solely on their self-reports that they cannot sleep because of depression or anxiety, because it cannot be established which occurred first.

A problem for the study of sleep disorders such as insomnia is that the scientific study of insomnia requires the use of polysomnography in a sleep laboratory. This technique is used to record all the biophysiological changes that occur in the body (e.g. EEG changes) over a night-time's sleep. A problem with this approach is that highly controlled studies such as this may lack ecological validity in that they do not generalize to other situations, particularly the circumstances in which the individual usually sleeps. For example, an individual may regularly sleep with another person, whose sleeping patterns contribute to the individual's sleeping difficulties.

In another good section of AO2, the student elaborates the problems associated with self-reports, as well as the general difficulties establishing the *direction* of any cause–effect relationship. There is good use of research evidence to support the arguments being developed. Research evidence also makes your answer more informed than speculative, so will always earn you higher marks for your evaluation (provided it is appropriate to the context of the material).

The answer ends with a good discussion of the problems of studying sleep disorders in the laboratory and so constitutes AO3 material (although this is credited under the more general AO2/AO3 marking allocations).

Strong answer: overall comment

This student has kept 'on task' throughout this question. They have structured their response to the exact requirements of the question, making sure that the AO1 and AO2 material is in the right proportions. It is accurate and well supported by evidence throughout, and is a clear Grade A.

Glossary

Adaptive   Term used to describe an evolved behaviour (or trait) that increases the likelihood of the individual's survival and successful reproduction

Autoimmune diseases   Conditions where the immune system fails to recognize the body's own tissues and attacks them, e.g. rheumatoid arthritis and Type 1 diabetes

Backwards rotation   A traditional pattern of shift work whereby individuals move from one shift to an earlier shift (e.g. an evening shift to a morning shift)

Body clocks   Common name for 'endogenous pacemakers', the genetically inherited mechanism whose role is to control biological rhythms

Cataplexy   A sudden loss of muscle tone leading to physical collapse even during waking hours (a symptom of narcolepsy)

Chronotype   An individual's stable pattern of sleep/waking; at the extremes are morning types ('larks') who wake earlier and go to sleep earlier, and evening types ('owls') who wake later but are happier going to sleep later

Circadian rhythms   Rhythmical cycles that have a full cycle of 24 hours or thereabouts, e.g. the human sleep/waking cycle

Comorbid   Indicating the presence of one or more disorders (or diseases) in addition to a primary disease or disorder

Concordance rate   In a sample of twin pairs, if one twin of each pair has a particular disorder, the concordance rate refers to the number of times that the other twin also shows that disorder; in a sample of 200 pairs of twins, if 90 have the disorder, then the concordance rate is 45 per cent

Correlational   Indicative of an association between two variables (but not indicating a cause-and-effect relationship)

Diathesis-stress model   A general model of disorders that proposes that people develop disorders (e.g. sleepwalking) when they possess both a constitutional vulnerability (diathesis) and are exposed to stressful events

Diurnal   Sleeping at night and awake in the daytime

Dyssomnia   Any disturbance or difficulty related to sleep, including problems falling asleep or staying asleep, as seen in insomnia, or disorders leading to excessive daytime sleepiness, such as sleep apnoea or narcolepsy

Ecological validity   The extent to which research findings can be generalized to other settings

Electroencephalogram (EEG)   In electro-encephalography, electrodes attached to the scalp record the electrical activity of the brain and allow researchers to classify different levels of arousal

Endogenous pacemakers   A genetically inherited mechanism whose role is to control biological rhythms; the scientific term for 'biological clock' or 'body clock' – 'endogenous' means 'internal', as opposed to 'exogenous' meaning 'external'

Exogenous   External (as opposed to 'endogenous' meaning 'internal')

Forwards rotation   A pattern of shift work whereby individuals move from one shift to a later shift (e.g. a morning shift to an evening shift)

Free-running studies   Research studies in which biological rhythms are allowed to run free in the absence of the usual external zeitgebers (especially light) that synchronize the endogenous pacemaker with the outside world

Homeostatic   The maintenance of a constant internal environment (e.g. body temperature)

Hormone   A chemical that travels in the blood and controls the actions of other cells or organs

Hypnagogic hallucinations   Auditory or visual hallucinations, rather like dreams, that occur particularly when just falling asleep or just waking up

Hypocretin   a protein in the brain that is involved in the regulation of sleep. People that have low levels of hypocretin often develop narcolepsy

Hypothalamus   An area of the brain lying a little behind the eyes that acts like a thermostat, making sure that bodily functions are maintained within tolerable limits

Infradian rhythms   Rhythmical cycles that last more than a day, e.g. the female menstrual cycle or the annual hibernation of animals

Insomnia   Problems with sleep patterns and, in particular, difficulties in sleep onset (falling asleep) or sleep maintenance

Jet lag   The effects produced through the disruption of biological rhythms following jet travel that crosses time zones; effects include tiredness, problems with attention, irritability and even anxiety

Melatonin   A hormone released from the pineal gland into the circulatory system that has actions on many structures in the brain and body; in particular, it influences many of the body's rhythmic activities

Narcolepsy   Narcolepsy is an unusual sleep disorder affecting around 1 in 2000 people characterized by excessive daytime sleepiness, cataplexy, hypnagogic hallucinations and sleep paralysis

Neurotransmitter   Chemical messengers (e.g. serotonin) that transmit nerve impulses from one nerve cell to another

Nocturnal   Sleeping in the daytime and active at night

Non-rapid eye movement sleep (NREM)   The four stages of sleep (1-4) outside of REM, during which the EEG is synchronized and the deep stages are dominated by large, slow delta waves

Phase advance   The situation where a person's biological clock gets behind local time (e.g. through West to East jet travel) and has to move forward ('advance') in order to catch up with local zeitgebers

Phase delay   The situation where a person's biological clock gets ahead of local time (e.g. through East to West jet travel) and has to 'delay', i.e. wait for external cues to catch up

Pineal gland   A small, pea-shaped gland in the middle of the brain that produces melatonin

Polysomnography   Use of multiple measures to obtain a full picture of all the physiological and behavioural events happening in sleep; measures may record brain activity, eye movements, body and limb movements, heart rate, blood pressure and levels of oxygen circulating in the blood

Primary insomnia   Insomnia with no obvious precipitating cause

Rapid eye movement sleep (REM)   A recurring sleep state during which the brain seems to have an aroused pattern, but the body muscles are paralysed; sleep is accompanied by rapid movements of the eyes and twitching of the extremities

Reductionist   An approach to behaviour that explains a complex set of facts, entities, phenomena or structures (e.g. human sleep/waking patterns) by another, simpler set (e.g. underlying biological mechanisms)

Replication   The repetition of a research study, generally with different situations and different subjects, to find out whether the basic findings of the original study can be generalized to other participants and circumstances

Restless legs syndrome (RLS)   A disorder of the part of the nervous system that affects movements of the legs; people with RLS have strange sensations in their legs (and sometimes arms) and an irresistible urge to move their legs to relieve the sensations. Because it usually interferes with sleep, it also is considered a sleep disorder

Retinohypothalamic tract   Pathway connecting the retina to the SCN, giving the SCN information about the amount of light reaching the retina from the outside world

Secondary insomnia   Insomnia with a clear precipitating cause, such as a medical condition or psychological disorder

Serotonin   A neurotransmitter; abnormal activity of serotonin has been linked to depression

Sleep apnoea   A sleep disorder characterized by abnormal pauses in breathing or instances of abnormally low breathing, during sleep

Sleep efficiency   Time in bed actually asleep

Sleep onset latency   The time taken to fall asleep

Somnambulism   When people leave their beds while still asleep and walk around as if awake

Somnotypology   An individual's sleep preferences in terms of circadian preference (chronotype) and amount of sleep needed

Suprachiasmatic nucleus (SCN)   A small region of the hypothalamus that is found just above the point where the optic fibres from each eye cross over and travel to the opposite hemisphere

Thalamus   An evolutionary ancient area of the forebrain sitting on top of the brain stem that largely determines how much sensory information reaches higher centres

Ultradian rhythms   Rhythmical cycles that last less than a day, e.g. sleep stages such as bouts of REM

Zeitgeber   'Time giver' stimuli that alter the biological clock on a daily basis. Examples include light and heat

Index

Index